Kiss Me Goodnight

Kiss Me Goodnight

STORIES AND POEMS BY WOMEN
WHO WERE GIRLS WHEN THEIR MOTHERS DIED

Edited by

Ann Murphy O'Fallon
Margaret Noonan Vaillancourt

SYREN BOOK COMPANY
Minneapolis

This book is dedicated to
Ethel Koelzer Murphy, Jeanne Buchanan Noonan,
and all the other mothers who die too young.

Contents

Contributors' Family Pictures

Thank you

This work is in your hands because of the hard work and support of many people.

Anna Warrrock and Bonnie West, you are the greatest! Thanks for standing by us throughout this journey and offering endless advice and counsel.

We also wish to thank Emily Anderson, Annette Bar-Cohen, Barb Clifton, Kathryn Daniels, Patricia Segal Freeman, Anne Gearity, Nora Hedling, Marge Higgins, Sissel Johannessen, Buzz Mandel, Meg Emmet Masterson, Maureen Murphy, Luanne Nyberg, David O'Fallon, Patricia Ohmans, Mary Rossi, Betty Ryan, Margaret Shryer, Deb Snell, Sandra Taylor, Becky Wildmo, and the staff at Syren Book Company for your incredible support and encouragement.

We give special thanks to our children, Chelsea, Erin, Brendan, and Caitlin. We love you!

Most of all we want to thank all the authors who submitted works to us. Whether their submissions were chosen or not, we applaud their part in this creation. Reading every poem and story touched our hearts.

Thank you one and all.

Ann and Margaret

Foreword

This project began when I looked up from my computer at work one day and saw a woman my age riding her bicycle into my cubicle. "Hi," she said, "my name is Margaret and I'll be your new neighbor."

We became friends, and shared stories and writing we had done. Margaret is a passionate writer, and I had spent years studying and working professionally in the area of grief and loss. As we got to know each other, one of the stories we shared was of our mothers' deaths. My mother died of breast cancer in 1956, leaving behind five children ages six through thirteen. I was the second youngest at age nine. Margaret's mother died from complications of alcoholism when Margaret was seventeen. Her older sister was in college and two younger siblings were in elementary school.

We both grew up in the Midwest in a time when parents were reluctant to talk over life's realities with their children. I knew my mother was seriously ill when we began to pray for her at school. I knew she was critically ill when the priest came to our house to give her the Last Sacrament. It was not something I talked about with her or my dad or anyone else. After she died we rarely spoke of her again.

I spent years searching to understand the profound residue of confusion, loss, and numbness carried forward within me following my mother's death. Throughout my life I met many women who, like Margaret, experienced their mothers' deaths as children, and my heart always opened to them. I felt we were members of a unique sisterhood.

One of the side effects of having your mother die when you are a child is the deep sense of feeling permanently different from your peers. Especially for girls longing to "fit in," this experience can be quite isolating. Many girls don't know if it is okay to talk about their mom's life or death to their friends and relatives. Few girls can find the words to talk about this experience and most have no one to listen.

As a psychologist I've facilitated many mother-loss therapy groups and have seen the bonds leap across the room as each participant shares the story of her mother's death. Within these groups I talked and I listened to each woman describe with powerful emotions her memories of her mom, of her mom's death, of the funeral, of life afterward. Many talked of how much the little girl inside her missed having her mother as a role model, someone to nurture and guide her thorough the difficulties of adult life. Many carried forward an idealized version of her mother and what she might be like if she were still alive. Some found therapy, writing, or other people to help them keep going. But every one carried deep within herself a tender, vulnerable spot for her mother, for what was and what might have been.

This kind of sharing has held the most powerful healing for me. Though each story is different, each woman's words about a mother loved or hated helped me feel a bit less alone. I could see that my story was one of many stories, that my story had a place in the collective human experience.

In this spirit, Margaret and I decided to gather together stories and poems written by women who shared our loss. We wanted to offer a collection of heartfelt writing to our readers so that they could perhaps find themselves within this poignant sisterhood. We wanted this book to come straight from the heart, without interpretation or analysis. We wanted to use the poetry and short stories we had amassed to give readers a window into the little girls these women once were, little girls faced with too big a trauma to understand, little girls without the vocabulary or maturity to express the deep emptiness they felt upon the deaths of their mothers.

One of our readers said, "Reading these works is like walking into a sacred place," and this is exactly what we hoped to accomplish. By reading the tender, soft, sometimes angry, sometimes funny, often painful works by our authors, one experiences the burden and the power of such incomprehensible and difficult emotions. The works in *Kiss Me Goodnight* take readers out of their heads and into their hearts, where healing may begin.

Many mothers around the world die each year leaving young daughters behind. As Hope Edelman and others have pointed out, the ability of these daughters to mourn and resolve their loss is compromised by the limitations of being a child. It is my hope that *Kiss Me Goodnight* opens the door to words, images, and feelings many motherless daughters find so very difficult to recognize, much less express. It is my hope that these writings resonate within the hearts of motherless daughters everywhere.

Ann Murphy O'Fallon
Minneapolis, Minnesota
September 2004

I am seventeen. I'm sitting in a chair gazing out at a family I believe is no longer mine. On the couch across from my chair there are two small children in their pajamas. The boy looks like my little brother, Topper, and the girl looks like my little sister, Jolley. They are squished into the sides of a sad-eyed man who is probably my father. Over there, in the archway to the dining room, is a young woman in the arms of a young man. She is sobbing into his chest. I think it is my older sister, Debbie, and her boyfriend, Ted, but I'm not certain because my mother has just died. I really only know one thing—I am alone and everyone else in the room has somebody. Left alone, I do the only thing possible: I tell myself I don't care because my mother was a drunk and she didn't love me anyway and besides I don't need anybody.

Forty years later, I meet Ann O'Fallon, the coeditor of *Kiss Me Goodnight,* and we become friends and share pieces we have written about our mothers' deaths. It is Ann's story that opens the possibility for me to look at my mother's death with adult eyes.

Ann and I are amazed at the impact our work has on each other. As we talk through our lives then and our lives now, we suddenly come to the same conclusion—to publish an anthology of stories and poems by women who were children when their mothers died. The one tiny ad we place brings forth a flood of submissions from hundreds of women.

For three years, like Ann, I read stories and poems from women who were girls when lung cancer, breast cancer, Nazis, heart attacks, alcohol, suicide, childbirth, and other agents of death robbed them of their mothers. I sit in a chair at night reading piece after piece after piece. What these women write makes me cry, makes me angry, makes me laugh, and makes me sad.

It also makes me hallucinate. After a while, the mothers seem to soak into my soul, my dreams, and my everyday life. I see a woman on the street and know it is the mother in a story I read the night before. I misplace another woman's poems and come to believe that her mother does not want the poems to be published. Once I am even sure I see this mother crouched in a corner of my closet with the poems crushed to her chest. I never muster up the courage to go into the closet and wrestle them away; but exact copies of these poems appear in this anthology along with the poems, stories, and pictures of fifty other women.

For three years, I have had the privilege to sit in a chair with *Kiss Me Goodnight* and be swept up by the courage, power, pain, humor, and support of the women whose stories and poems you, too, now hold. It is because of these women that I have found the courage to look into the heart of that seventeen-year-old girl who sat in a chair all alone on the night of her mother's death. It is because of the women in this book that I am no longer alone. My hope is that *Kiss Me Goodnight* can do for others what it has done for me.

Margaret Noonan Vaillancourt
Minneapolis, Minnesota
September 2004

Introduction

If you are a child when your mother dies, the unimaginable has happened. You travel alone to a continent of grief no one else can ever find. In that land, your loneliness is complete, your longing for a mother holds you captive, sometimes for years. You are changed by that travel. You know now that disasters happen and without any warning of how deeply you will hurt. It feels as if you will hurt forever, and now you know what forever means. You are five, or seven, or thirteen, or eighteen. As have the women in *Kiss Me Goodnight,* you must make your way through a landscape that can never again be called normal.

Sometimes as you travel you are fearful no one will find you. You think your brief experience of a mother is unique, so that it cannot—or should not—be shared. Your shame—how could you lose your mother!—tastes like salt. Your anger at her for leaving makes you doubly ashamed. Whether she was brutal or loving, whether it happened quickly or over years. Whether you were close to her, or not; whether you did everything together, or you were the forgotten child. She is gone.

My mother's absence changed my dreams. Things others could take for granted I would never have and could never imagine. My mother would never read my book report, buy me a party dress, watch me play hockey, meet my boyfriend, meet my life. I would never know what it's like to talk as an adult to my mother. This created a second split, another push apart from ordinary people. So I began to write down what details I knew and to imagine the details I didn't know. Though I will live always with questions, I have learned to keep writing until the answers that come—become true.

How grateful I am to read the strength in *Kiss Me Goodnight.* The women in this book have come back from that continent to give us their stories and poems, to sketch the jagged geography of grief from mother-loss. In these stories, it's clearly possible that an evil force has decapitated a father and put his head in the glove compartment of his truck. Why not? It's as feasible as losing a mother. Or the daughter decides that a tragic air is best, putting it on thick, because it feels better to make it an act, and it's easier that way, to pretend, while the anger flares like distress beacons of a sinking ship. Daughters watch other adults do strange things, throw out the mother's belongings (but can't a daughter keep something of hers?) or refuse permission to be a cheerleader (a mother would have given it), and a daughter's powerlessness without a mother—even to argue with—cuts paths of despair inside her. If she's young enough, she might become convinced there's been a mistake, and any moment her dead mother will rise up. Only the daughter can't believe that for long, she's too smart, really—and as the church bell tolls, she moves from age nine to adult in three minutes. Another child talks to her mother's inert, dying body in the hospital. She brings wild flowers and puts them in a bedside cup. She holds her hand, not worried that her mother doesn't answer as she chatters about a neighbor's rooster. No one has said her mother isn't coming home—of course she is. The wild flowers will be the first thing she sees when she wakes up.

As these writers face their grief, no detail is missed, or spared, or too ugly to remember: the gurgles of illness, the smell of a sick room, the coffin, a coat, a dress—often the women speak of their mothers' dresses, as if memory of a dress preserves a mother's form. The value in these details comes from the enormous questioning that has only these small pieces left from which to make a world.

Yet the women in *Kiss Me Goodnight* write beyond themselves. Uncompromising and brave, they tell us all what it's like to survive the sadness and despair, the joy taken away and the love denied. It may sound simplistic, but grief requires grieving, which means discovering the staying power and the guts to go on, and the stories and poems in this book are the detailed road maps back to the land of the living.

You bake a pie and feel your mother's hands helping you, though you never baked a pie with her. You make a decision to become a prison warden instead of a ballerina, and you know she would have applauded your choice, despite the dance lessons, because she wanted you to be happy. If she had known, that's what she would have wanted you to do.

My hope is that the courage of women whose despair becomes not a sappy love, but a love that holds life and death together will give courage to others lost on the continent of grief, whether because of a mother's death, or that of a spouse, a sibling, a child. There is a way back. These daughters are the storytellers who will guide your journey.

Anna M. Warrock
Somerville, Massachusetts
August 2004

Kiss Me Goodnight

Ellen was 15 when her mother, Catherine
Mahoney Wade, died of cancer in 1972.

August 1999: Light Is a Measure of Time

Scientists have found the oldest
point in the universe: a galaxy filled
with new stars and all day long
I've been thinking about my mother.
How long it has been since
the nun came to fetch me from class
so I could wait for my brother to take me home,
even though I was in trouble
for using *CliffNotes* in my Macbeth paper.
I practiced driving on the way,
Jack tossed the keys to me, figuring, perhaps,
concentration would hold us together.
All of us kids orbited around
her bed. I drove pretty good, I said
and she told me, "That's nice, honey,
now go get something to eat."

This new galaxy, the paper says,
looks young to scientists because
the deeper they look back in space,
the further they look back in time.
When I look back, I see her
bald as an irradiated nestling,
not silver-haired and regal, not the young
woman with the finger-waved Marcel who smiles
from the photo in the scrapbook.

This new galaxy may look as it was
a few billion years after the Big Bang
so scientists are trying to see how worlds form,
how we coalesce from the sea of light elements.
My father and mother met reaching
for a piece of banana cream pie
at the cafeteria of the Edgewater
Laundry where they worked.

Along with the Hubble, astronomers use
a spectrograph and computers to separate
overlapping images and uncover the distant galaxy.
One day she'd wear blue shoes, the next,
the pumps were black so she'd call from her closet,
asking would I be a good girl and transfer
things to her matching pocketbook.
I'd put in her wallet, the chintzy eyeglass and cigarette
cases, the lipstick worn to a parabola,
only tobacco bits, bobby pins,
or a sticky red pill left in the lining.

This oldest galaxy is called Sharon,
after the sister of one of the astronomers.
My mother and I have the same middle name: Marie.
Through the myopic lens of memory, I see mother,
the shopping bag of library books at her feet.
She glances up from the pages to watch with me
Laugh-In, Burke's Law, or *Man from U.N.C.L.E.*
those waves still lingering somewhere perhaps.

It is not often I consider the heavens,
physics, or universal truths
but today it consoled me to think time never breaks
nor does light stop, but continues.

**CHRISTINE BOLLERUD**

Christine was four when her mother,
Ruth Fulde Bollerud, died in a
traffic accident in 1966.

It's just a purse but . . .

I bought a purse yesterday. I'm sure the people at Macy's were giving me strange looks but I didn't care. I found a black purse that is kind of old fashioned. It has two little metal round clasps that snap against each other to keep the purse closed.

This kind of black purse reminded me of the one my mother had (she died when I was four) and when she closed it, it made this deep clack that I loved to hear.

I remember opening her purse. It smelled like Chanel No. 5 and Juicy Fruit gum. It always held nervous wads of red, lipstick-stained tissue and a black fountain pen and her wallet with her passport picture in it.

I would sit on her lap or by her feet on the floor opening her purse just so I could snap it closed. I would do this over and over just to hear that clacking sound.

Well, yesterday I found a display of purses with this style of clasp. I spent twenty minutes going to each purse—opening and closing it until I found the one that made that sound.

That sound—a deep, primal, comforting clacking that makes me four years old again—even if just for a second.

The Mother Thing

I pretend
To be whole
To be healed
But my heart
Leaks a squishy
Squashy question
That comes out
In tears—the mother thing

I tell people it's
Something else
I'm premenstrual
I'm creative
Anything but—the mother thing

No matter my resolve
Not to let it float up
From its sodden grave
The question leaks out
In tears—
"Did you love me, Mommy?"

Jeanne was 17 when her mother, Wilma
Ruth Stiles, died suddenly following a
seizure and high fever in 1969.

Fairies Live in the Next Town

Bunny beats all her brothers and sisters to the pink bathroom. Her heart pounds like a racehorse coming down the final stretch of the quarter-mile. Washing her face, she scrubs hard. Today, it must shine. Thank heavens, it's not her period. No pimples. The mirror's cloudy, a crack at the bottom is held together with dirty brown masking tape. A wrinkled swan decal nests in the upper left-hand corner. It covers a spot where her brother, Lester, shot it with his BB gun. That was four years ago when Bunny was eleven. Before her periods. Before her daddy divorced his second wife, Bunny's first stepmother. Before Bunny had taken her shirt off and let Duke Richards put his mouth on her titties.

Bunny's thick, caramel hair flows down her back. She wants to wear it long and loose like Rita Hayworth, but her new stepmother, Mona, screams at her everyday, "Get that horse's mane up in a gum band." It gives Bunny a headache: the ponytail and Mona's yelling. Mona won't even let Bunny wear a bra. So, Bunny's breasts are not grapefruits. In the ninth grade, girls don't go around flopping. Bunny wears a long slip to hide her breasts under her dresses. There's no predicting when her hard nipples will push against thin cotton blouses. Duke says he likes it when she's cold.

"Hurry up, Bunny. Yeah, you're not the only one who has school. C'mon, Bunny, I have to pee." Like tree limbs banging a window in a storm, the voices of her brothers and sisters rush her brushing her teeth.

Bunny's stomach bounces inside her. It takes turns doing flips with her heart. Today the cheerleading squad tryouts are at lunchtime, and Bunny has made it to the finals. Eighty-five girls started. Sixteen are left. Seven will be chosen. More than anything, Bunny wants to wear a cheerleading sweater. More than letting her hair down. More than wearing a bra. More than marrying Duke.

Mona doesn't want Bunny to do anything but baby-sit and clean houses for women who advertise for help in the papers. Mona won't let Bunny's sisters go to dances or her brothers play Little League. Mona bleaches her hair and chain-smokes. Every morning she paints her nails. By nine A.M., Mona starts the laundry and drinking. By noon her voice is shrill and demanding. By four, Bunny's daddy comes home. "Baby, let me tell you about my day," Mona starts. "Here, let me show you how high the clothes were piled in the hallway. See here, I broke a nail on the dryer's door. Honey, we got to do something about these kids wearing so many clothes. Christ, I can't have a nice dinner for you when I spend all day being a slave for them. Baby, bring me a cold one and give Mama a kiss." Mona presses herself against Bunny's daddy and pinches him where his trouser zipper ends. It makes him crazy.

After a few beers, Bunny's daddy jumps on the bandwagon. "You brats quit dirtying so many clothes. Can't you have a little respect for Mona? What you think she is? She ain't even your mama. But she's doing everything for you but wiping your sorry little asses. I want you to shape up, pick up, and show her some respect." By then, he's kissing Mona and feeling under her blouse while Bunny and the kids try to eat Mona's burned meatloaf and sorry soup beans.

u

Constantly, Bunny practices cheers. When she takes out the garbage, she does jumps until both her legs are higher than the metal cans. Before gym class, she rehearses the claps. Bunny whispers chants to herself, sees herself on the football field under the lights, in front of the crowd, her orange sweater with its tiger face, her pompoms shaking in her fists. She asks the girls who study dance to teach her how to do splits. Duke likes to watch her do splits and cartwheels. He says, "Baby, when you gonna do a split with me?" Duke. After she'd let him take pictures of her in her bikini, he gave her a charm bracelet. He was going to the army soon, and then they'd be married, live somewhere far away from Mona and her daddy. Somewhere warm. Maybe Texas. Maybe Florida. Yes, Florida would be nice. Palm trees and sand. Bunny could wear her bikini. Duke could rub her back with suntan lotion. Duke has nice hands, and when his tongue parts her teeth, she feels sort of drunk and warm all over.

u

Bunny stuffs the black-and-white checkered shorts into her blue notebook, takes a deep breath, and leaves Mona screaming about burned toast smelling up the house. Bunny can do very well without breakfast at her house. A glass of milk is plenty. Good mornings had gone the way of cooked oats and brown sugar and her mother's sleepy smile. She bites her lower lip. She cannot think about her mother today. Not now. In the morning fog, she moves to a rhythm of sideline cheers. Her step is so fast she almost forgets to turn off at her friend's house.

Her friend's house is Irish. Catholic. The blessed mother guards their flowerbed, and a crucifix with a dried palm necklace hangs in the kitchen. People there laugh and bump over and around each other like colored balls on a pool table. Her friend's mother is plump and freckled and smiles in a shy way that makes Bunny feel welcome. Sometimes, Bunny's friend complains about the Friday fish or the cookies or the apples being too big in her lunch. Bunny wants to tell her about Mona and how she makes them all pack their own lunches the night before school—stale bread and bargain peanut butter, cookies so hard they could be used as blocks to build a bridge. Apples never happen. "Too expensive," Mona says. Mona needs money for cigarettes and blue eye shadow and go-go boots and beer.

Every day, Bunny watches her friend's mother kiss the kids goodbye. "Ma, enough with the kissing. I'm fourteen already. I ain't no baby." Her friend complains.

"Lay off," Bunny tells her when they head out the door.

"What?"

"Just lay off. So, your mother wants to kiss you. So what?"

"So I'm fourteen. I don't need her slobbering on me like I'm a baby."

"Like a kiss will hurt your head? Your thick head?" Bunny grins.

"Yeah. Like maybe it will."

"Dumb."

"Look, she can kiss the little kids. I just don't want her kissing me."

"She likes to."

"I don't give a shit."

"You're mean."

"Drop it."

"OK, but your mother can't help being sweet. You told me she was gonna be a nun once right? See, she can't help it. She's full of kindness."

"Yeah, whatever."

"Want Mona?"

"No thanks."

"Sure? I'll trade. I'll even throw in my record player."

"That bitch? No way. You scared about tryouts?"

"A little."

"You got Kathy and Mary beat. Their splits stink. And Alice, she does all right until there's a crowd. You know."

"Yeah."

"Mrs. McHenry likes you."

"Yeah, but that's one vote."

"Will Duke be there?"

"Oh yeah." Bunny sighs.

"You better be careful."

"Or what?"

"You know. Ray Ann's sister is pregnant."

"So?"

"So, it happens. I'm just saying I never seen a cheerleader with a big belly."

"Yeah. Well, we haven't done it. Yet."

"Yeah, but everything else."

"You don't know it all. Duke loves me."

"Yeah. Duke's a senior."

"So?"

"So, he's been around. My ma says boys do stuff, with girls, with lots of girls. Then, they walk away. I just want you to be careful, Bunny." Bunny's friend has a forehead full of pimples, and she hunches forward because she's tall and has large breasts.

"Duke won't do anything with anybody but me. I should know. He gave me this bracelet didn't he? It's just one step away from his class ring."

"I'm just saying be careful."

"Just drop it."

"OK."

"I have to make it for cheerleader."

"OK."

They walk on in silence: the unpretty girl who knows about boys and the pretty one who knows about Duke. Behind them, the housing projects are connected by streets wound in coils, and women's lives are lived quietly inside crowded rooms that are books with pasty gray endings. The milkman comes, and the mailman, and, once in a while, an encyclopedia salesman. Children are born and outgrow their shoes and get married. Mothers paint their kitchens and thin metal cupboards over and over; they shake rugs and dust mops and jars of change. Fathers work at the mills and drink to forget the hell of a blast furnace. In darkness, children learn to kneel. There are the old prayers and stories about a girl with long hair in a tower and another one who wears glass slippers, but fairies live in the next town and Snow White died, so women here seldom eat apples.

u

Bunny can see her face. Smiling. A happy face. Not the kind she uses to please her teachers or get Mona off her back. No. The kind a person gets when battle is over and won. Clean white tennis shoes, folded-down bobby socks. Flipping over in a black pleated skirt, landing straight up. Bunny in the center of the gym. Bunny on top of the cheerleading pyramid. Bunny jumping straight out, straight up. She closes her metal locker. At lunchtime she'll be back to grab her shorts and head for the locker room.

She can't answer the last three questions on the English quiz. Hemingway's short story "Fifty Grand." Why should Bunny care about the boxer? He was done for. He got beat up really bad. He wanted to be with his family. So what? What was the story's point? Money? She didn't have money unless she worked. And then there was Mona telling her she had to buy her winter coat and penny loafers. Mona. Now, she'd love to put her in the ring with the boxer, and she'd pay more than fifty grand to watch him pound the living shit out of her.

When the third bell rings, Bunny closes her eyes and says a prayer. Her friend's mother says *prayer never hurts*. (She was almost a nun, so she should know.) Bunny's government teacher, Mr. Butler, steps close to her desk, clears his throat. "You OK, Bunny?"

"Yeah, I'm fine. I've gotta run."

u

The locker room blooms a sweet, smelly cloud of hair spray and rainbows of new striped pastel short sets. Bunny tries not to care that her dumb checkered shorts are faded from so many washings. Her palms are cool and sweaty; her mouth, dry. She wiggles into her shorts and that phony smile and runs out into the gym.

Duke slouches in the front row. His black hair's slicked back in a DA. His cigarettes hide in the sleeve of his T-shirt, and his slender legs open in a "V." He winks at Bunny and points to his ring.

Mrs. McHenry walks to the microphone. "The girls will each do two cheers. After all the girls are done, the votes will be counted. The winners will be posted this afternoon. Good luck."

Bunny's name is called. Duke's is the only face Bunny sees. His blue eyes. She puts her body into motion. It becomes hot fudge sliding down vanilla ice cream. The height and stretch of her jumps are awesome. Her splits—great. (The girls who took dance classes will say that later.) When she finishes both cheers, she smiles at Duke. She honest-to-God smiles—the beam of a winner. She has that feeling inside her, the one she gets when she knows the test she's just handed in deserves an "A." That feeling becomes a sail, which carries her through the afternoon. The list will be posted by the end of the day. Then Bunny will know.

u

Sixteen girls swarm the bulletin board outside the principal's office. They are bees coming to a hive. Some of the girls swear, some cry, others remain quiet. Bunny waits. She waits until Kathy and Mary and Alice are three shadows by the water fountain at the end of the hall. She swallows hard and walks to the faded green board.

BUNNY LARSON. Her name is typed. It is right there. Typed. All capital letters. Her name. BUNNY LARSON. A cheerleader. So, God listens. So, her friend's mother, who was almost a nun, was right. Her tall friend with the pimpled face is beside her now, hugging her, giving her a kiss. Bunny cries. She doesn't like to, but she cries, and then (to herself) she says a sort of thank-you prayer.

Duke drives her home in his faded red Falcon. He buys her a strawberry milkshake from the Dairy Dream. He puts his hand inside her blouse and rolls her left nipple between his fingers and thumb. It feels so good. Today everything feels good. Bunny lets Duke put his smoky tongue in her mouth when he kisses her goodbye.

Mona meets her at the door; she squawks, "I'm telling your daddy that boy's driving you home and kissing you on the mouth."

"You're drunk, Mona. Get out of my way." Mona slaps Bunny, hard, in the face. Bunny shoves her.

"You can't talk to me that way. Wait till your daddy gets home. You little brat." Mona weaves her way to the sink.

Bunny pushes past Mona's bad breath and the pot full of gluey potatoes she's tried to cook for supper. Bunny goes to her room to listen to the Supremes sing, "Baby, Baby, Baby, Where Did Our Love Go."

u

Three days later, at the meeting for new cheerleaders, Mrs. McHenry asks Bunny to please stay. Mrs. McHenry looks like a girl herself in the blue cotton skirt and carefully ironed blouse with the red sailboats floating over her breasts. "Bunny, your stepmother called the office today. She said she didn't know anything about you trying out for cheerleader. She said you did all this—without permission. That you didn't have time for the games or money for uniforms. I'm really sorry, Bunny. I tried to talk to her, but she said even your father was against this. Without parental permission . . ." Her voice trailed off. It floated somewhere far away with those pretty sailboats on her blouse.

Standing there in her sister's corduroy jumper, braless, with her hair pulled so tight in a ponytail, Bunny fell backward in her mind. She landed in a room where her mother was still alive, smiling in her red lipstick, church hat, and dotted yellow dress. A magic place where Bunny's small finger pointed to gingerbread men inside the glass case, and her mother handed the baker dime after dime.

Janet was three when her mother,
Margaret, died from cancer in 1958.

This Is How I Like My Eggs

I'm vacuuming those old regrets.
My mother's death,
a sliver in a swollen hand.
I can spot her sectioned smile,
a piece of fruit canned by time
and squeamishness of Father's grief.
He chews it in the midnight hour
when no one knows his tears
are icebergs sinking ships
that act as though they own the sea.
Reefs he's lived, their haggard rocks
calmed by beer, massaged by crazy busyness—
their currents, jars of unspread jam—
colors fading with his flesh.
Sitting on demise's lip,
afraid to put his toes in rivers
deeper than his waist of strength.

This model of a leaving car—
throttle rushing through a sun—
fumes and flames contained in dampers
of this courage plastic in its certainty.
My body craves a different shape:
the open egg on crackling skillets,
sunny up and sporting yolk,
not rotted, rolled behind a couch.
Here with you, I pick a lock,
blow the dust off diaries

bolted with their rusted lies.
Here with you, I nurse the
wingless birds of fate
where legs were tarnished candlesticks
and diaries of shaking shame.

Wild Horses, Sugar Cubes

Father took his strength too far
denying that you left in death.
I was only three back then—
don't remember how it felt
to smell your scent on apron strings,
on Sunday ties your perfume
must have rubbed against.
My sister took your tube of lipstick,
wrote some sad obscenity
across the steaming bathroom mirror.
He cleaned it up so quietly,
ruddy oil of tortured flesh
our innocence could not accept.
I run my finger over photos, thinking
of these middle years you never saw.
Memory is blinder than the blackest bat;
poetry is pressing pins in voodoo dolls
whose nerves are never recognized.

My hair is graying. Yours was not.
Its silky deep mahogany
that lit the doom and then dissolved.
I'll never know his heaviness,
arms like sacks of wet concrete

in sickened caves of lonely beds—
reaching for you
in interminable night—
sticking to his hollow loss
like ice cubes thaw and freeze again.
Two girls to raise without
the sutures of your palms
made certain that the wound you were
grew its scars, but never closed.
Our faces in the morning light—
sugar cubes an offering
to fetid tongues of wild horses
standing at the grieving trough.

Aching Vacancy

I was only three years old
when cancer's ugly dinosaur
ate contents of my father's joy,
left his mattress and his heart
a lopsided saddle with bruises
and cracks, a fact of life
to ride regardless of the heat.
With empty scrapbooks in my pen,
I do not grieve your death
in normal, comprehensive ways.

Its aching vacancy exists.
I cannot argue its point,
but have no real grist for poetry,
except the sand of a sealed urn.
Photos steeped in sepia

are grass clippings
in a smelly can my fingers
hate to rifle through.

I've thought of you on nights of proms:
you'd buff my shoes,
paint my toenails in the dark,
teach me how to kiss a man,
thread a needle, shape a pie.
I've thought of you on wedding days:
you'd have a hair brush in your hand,
comb the knots of nervous tangles
settled near moist baby's breath.

Leper spots of sadness sit
with venom in their secret moles.
My love for you a stringless harp
on stages of unopened plays.
The copyright of your morning smile
belongs to God or rings
around agnostic moons.
I wish I knew your apron bows.
Had your scent in borrowed sweaters
piled on and buttoned up
when times were ice and I was cold.

Barbara was eight when her mother,
Lee Gianni Magaldi, died of cancer.

Before My Birthday

I.

I brought the blue blanket for us to sit on.
It smelled salty like Ocean Beach.
My mother carried two white pots.

We spread the blanket and
snapped ends from string beans
freshly picked from our garden.

Enough to fill a big paper bag
enough for supper
with some to jar for winter.

If we canned a little from each picking, she said,
we'd have green beans to eat
when the garden rests.

We talked about
my eighth birthday party.
She asked what I wanted for a gift.

But we never filled the pots or finished the talk.
My mother's fingers trembled and her face was pale.
I knew the ambulance would come soon.

The screen door slammed closed behind her,
so hard I was afraid
it wouldn't open to let her back out.

Don't worry momma
you'll be home
in time for my birthday.

II.

The man in the gray hat helps me in the car.
It's bigger than ours.
My dad gets in but he's far away.

He doesn't look at me. The door slams shut.
Every lock clicks at once. We're sealed in.
We drive down our street.

My forehead is numb, pressing against the window.
Cars behind us have their lights on.
Don't they know it's morning?

We pass by our house without stopping.
People carry dishes to the door.
A lady with a basket is in our garden.

Don't touch that last row of green beans,
Momma said. *They won't be ready.*
Not until after my birthday.

Camincha was 14 when her mother
died of a broken heart.

An Announced Death

In your hand, la adivina had said. She had seen it in her hand. This line, see this line, this one here? Mamacita looked: That line? La adivina might as well have been showing her a road map. And la adivina knew it. But she had learned what was effective. Theatrics paid very well. So Mamacita did see his image spreading over her hand. Because he was twenty years her senior, it had to be him la adivina was referring to when she said, There is going to be a death in your family.

NEW DRUG TO AMAZE THE WORLD
Penicillin: Miracle Cure for Tuberculosis?

Mrs. Polar said it is fine to borrow the paper so long as Liliana returns it before Mr. Polar gets home. The printed word flares her imagination with her best girlfriend, Eileen. Together they make adventurous plans. They are going to be private secretaries, they are studying shorthand and typing. They are going to rent their own apartment. Like in the movies. Meantime, Liliana and her mother share a small house with Eileen, Eileen's oldest sister, Jessie, and their mother, la gringa Mae. Under February's summer sun the back patio is hot. Miraflores is experiencing a heat wave. Liliana looks up, the empty clotheslines hang limp. The blue sky shows no clouds. She gives up her seat on the bleached-out trunk and, holding *El Comercio,* goes to the spotless aromatic kitchen, empty in midafternoon. Cool because of the tile floor, cement walls, skylight. Her favorite place to read, daydream. I'll tell Mamacita, a cure, a miracle is coming to rescue us. Gracias, gracias, Virgen del Carmen. Liliana grabs the page, her finger pokes right through it. Oh! Mrs. Polar! Panicking, she tries smoothing it out. Her heart pounding, her eyes swallowing the words. Anguish, lately her constant companion, gives way to the old state of hope.

. . . in a few years this deadly disease might be wiped off the face of the Earth. Especially countries in Asia and Latin America will then know years of great prosperity. . . .

So it's coming, this penicillin. If only we could have it now. We could go back to our house. Pay the clinic so they won't send any more henchmen who threaten to haul away the living room furniture. Already everything else worth anything has been sold. Anguish returns.

u

Her mother and Jessie . . . their voices, their steps on the brick walk that borders the tiny front garden, and soon Jessie is in her bedroom, changing.

Liliana follows her mother into the dining/living room. Mamacita, I have something to tell you. Her mother, sitting down, eyes closed, head resting on her left hand, doesn't respond but halfway lifts her right arm toward her. Liliana cuddles in the warm curve of her body, enjoying her sweet fragrance. Then her mother looks into her eyes.

What's that strange look on your face, Mamacita, this mix of tenderness, guilt? Liliana wants to ask, but her mother closes her eyes again, resting from the trip to downtown Lima. Not to worry. They'll soon tell me what they've been up to. These women just love to talk. My news can wait. Isn't like it's going to happen today. But that look? At moments the thought of her death is more than she can stand. Losing her mother!

At fourteen life is piling up surprises on her. This anguish is one—new, disturbing. And in some ways so are the others, her changing face, body, the way people act around her lately, men, boys, the other girls' mothers. What do they see? And now Mamacita is also acting strange.

Suddenly she is saying, He was good . . . at moments. He had his moments. . . .

What? Liliana can't believe it. She wants to shout, Mamacita, what are you saying? My father, good?

Her mother goes on. Digging into her memories for anything good he had ever done or said.

Liliana keeps her thoughts to herself. Have you forgotten, Mamacita? I know it would upset you if I remind you. You see, I know. His cruelty. Burning your bundle of letters from Abuelita. Didn't you find him celebrating a bonfire in the yard, ordering the terrified houseboy to keep the fire burning? Laughing at your impotence, your frustration, your pain. Letters so dear to you. Her words carried the comfort you needed, Abuelita Echeyen understood. And his trying to bribe me for months, sending me messages: Liliana, you are welcome in my house, your own room, money to spend, new clothes. Come live with me. He just wants to hurt you. He knows you need me. He knows I'm your right arm—appointments, housework, errands. I used to adore him, returning the adoration he lavished on me. Now I feel only hate.

Jessie comes to sit with them. Liliana remembers she had something to share. But Jessie, like her mother, has a strange look on her face. She has changed from her street clothes, and next to the faded housedress her lips still full of lipstick look out of place. I'm going next week, get me a reading when I get my bonus check. I want her to tell me about the trips I'm going to make, she says in a low voice. And as if trying to hold an image in place, puts her head back, eyes closed, a smile on her lips.

Who is going to tell you what? Liliana asks, trying not to show how exasperated she is. Oh! Adult women! She gets up to open the window. A sweet breeze laced with perfume of dahlias and sweet peas joins them.

La adivina.

La . . . aren't they expensive? Liliana is surprised.

I treated her, Jessie says, smiling. The redheaded, beautiful Jessie. Twenty, una gringita born in Peru. Tall, freckled, angel face. Her brother, Richard, gone to live in Panama, from where he would continue to Europe. Jessie and her sister, Eileen, are hoping to be as lucky, to see the world.

Liliana positions herself on the edge of the chair. This beautiful person unfolding like a flower in front of her eyes fascinates her. Jessie wears makeup. Cuts her hair in styles imitating those in women's magazines!

Might even go to Europe someday to live. Liliana leans forward to better listen. Her news can wait.

Jessie looks at her sideways, teasingly, drinking in her admiration, and repeats, Trips . . .

Liliana pleads, To where?

Her mother smiling openly now: La adivina didn't say. It's up to the person!

Women's talk!

Her mother and Jessie go on and on. About la adivina, and what la adivina said. Then her mother, her eyes a pool of mixed feelings, brings Liliana into the conversation. One minute dry with a faraway look, moist the next. Her voice breaking under the weight of her emotions. He isn't . . . has probably not been in good health. . . . He used to . . . he had ulcers. Remember, Liliana? Oh! Her eyes moist again.

Liliana doesn't answer. Mamacita, are you talking about the man who has never been a husband, a father? Are those tears for him? Didn't we just see him on his way to collect rent from his apartment buildings? Without even looking our way?

Her mother again: La adivina told me, Liliana, that she sees a death in the family, her voice breaking. Begging her to understand, Mi hijita . . . ?

Liliana would like to tell her, Mamacita, why are you sorry for him? We don't even have money to buy the medicine you need or to take you to the doctor. This contagious disease ravaging your body makes you shake, cry. Makes you afraid I'll get it too, for it killed my uncle, my grandmother. You became an orphan at eight. He isn't helping us. And you get thinner, weaker every day.

But her mother looks away from Liliana, from what she sees in her eyes, the concerns filling the room, pressing against her.

Liliana says nothing.

u

The seed has been planted. Liliana plays with the thought—a thrill—that he will die. The catharsis of death. The severance. The adjusting of accounts. The coming to terms. The avenger. But did she know who it had come for? Meantime she watched over her mother, whose cheeks burned a dark rose. A product of the fever rising. Her eyes shining with it too. A pretty picture, maybe, but for the lips, parched, dry. Those fatal symptoms only look enticing, romantic on heroines of well-written fantasies. Mimi in *La Bohème,* Marguerite Gaultier in *The Lady of the Camelias.*

u

Aldo met the twenty-one-year-old nurse, the woman of the chaste, enormous brown eyes, with the hairdo of the deep wave over the right eye, at La Clínica Americana while visiting Lola, his cousin who was post-operative from appendicitis. The forty-four-year-old entrepreneur, Aldo Echeyen, nicknamed Don Juan, had seen something in that nurse . . . in the chaste, enormous brown eyes. He wanted to explore further . . . her soul. Be the first . . . the one to set it on fire. After all, he knew about chaste women . . . what there was under the surface, he had always found worth his time.

What is her name? he asked his cousin.

I don't know, Lola answered curtly. She knew Aldo. He married in-experienced pretty women, had kids with them all. Cultivated mistresses. Abandoned one family after another, disappearing overnight, taking the bait, the jewelry, to use on his next adventure.

Liliana has heard the tales about her father. Knows them to be true, for at that very moment he is living with his latest affair. Two kids already.

Painful years since he abandoned us, Mamacita. And you couldn't go back to nursing. The tuberculosis was discovered at the clinic in a routine health check. Positive!

u

The little one-bedroom house on Apurimac Street that slept eight would never be the same since the great caballero came in the three-piece gray flannel suit, the derby hat, the pearl-and-gold tiepin, the Swiss gold watch, the diamond ring. He dazzled them. They felt honored.

Later they learn of the suffering his womanizing caused, his constant badgering, taunting you with what he saw as your inability to be a society lady. Humiliating you, what had been petite became "too short," your chaste brown eyes "empty." The silent treatment. His absences when you, in pain, Mamacita, in anguish, stretched the few soles left till they became centavos. Pawned, sold whatever you could to buy groceries. Then that time I got violently ill in the middle of the night and you wrapped me in blankets, whisked me to the emergency. You paid the kind doctor who saved my life with your prized stamp collection. And Mamacita, you gave up the house we love, our house you worked so hard for. Renting it out would bring us an income, you said. But inflation ruined that. And missing our home is adding to your pain. And your health has not improved as a result of our living in three rooms rented from la gringa Mae. Tenaciously you cling to "I'll get well." Well, I have something I want to tell. . . .

But her mother is still at, Poor man, who would have thought? As if he had already died and they were visiting him at the funeral parlor. Liliana bites her tongue.

u

The three-piece suit, the derby hat, the pearl-and-gold tiepin, the Swiss gold watch, the diamond ring came back. He walked into the one-bedroom house at Apurimac Street that now sleeps one more, since Mamacita's family gave shelter to Liliana the little orphan, as she is always introduced.

Liliana hears his voice from the back patio where she just read MIRACLE CURE IS HERE: PENCILLIN in her uncle Jorge's *El Comercio*. Her father has come after Mamacita's Christian burial, given to her by her family. He came to claim "his daughter." Liliana overhears Uncle Jorge talking to her great-auntie, the one who raised Mamacita.

We have to let her go, he has rights, he is the father.

Liliana tells Uncle Jorge, I don't want to see him.

Great-auntie, crying, comes looking for her, holds her in her arms. Go in, your father is waiting for you. She obeys, her uncles, aunts, cousins all there in the living room.

In his most courtly manner her father gets up for Liliana. His smile turns radiant as his eyes take in the signs of her womanhood. He embraces her, speaking in a low voice as if just the two of them are in the room, You know why I chose today . . . ?

Liliana feels the loss like never before. Anguish fills her soul, her mind, her body. She stares at the floor. Does not speak.

Because I remembered you are fifteen today. Happy birthday, mi hijita! You are coming with me.

JUDITH DANIEL

*Judith was one in 1939 when
her mother, Margaret Bloom, died
from a streptococcal infection.*

A Mirror and a Photograph

My mother I don't remember, who died
when I was two
had just this vacant look, glazed,
that greets me in the mirror.

I remember a photo from a hunting trip.
She is about twenty-eight and
sits on a log like a girl on a piano stool,
smiles at the lens as though it separates
by light years
the viewer from the viewed.

Her vision stops so far inside
the camera's eye
I cannot catch her, but I see
it was a cold November morning
by the way she hugs her jacket tightly to her.

KATHRYN DANIELS

*Kathryn turned 12 the day after
her mother, Beatrice Alper Daniels,
succumbed to cancer in 1967 at age 42.*

At the End

She lay on the bed like a baby
steel bars reining her in
whittled to my weight
parched yellow skin
and fingernails Yes I'll take Latin
in seventh grade I'll
keep playing the piano
anything you say
just stay
then one day
she did not know me

Litany

Don't step on the cracks
or you'll
Don't step on the cracks
Don't step
Don't

One wrong move
and you'll
One wrong move

Don't step on the cracks
Don't

Don't make it my fault
Don't put it on my back
Don't put
Don't step
Don't

Untitled

Something had been bugging me
all day   someone had sat on my glasses
at school and broke them and I
cried all day even though it was
really no big deal but I kept saying
my mother's sick, it'll make an
extra trip   the other kids just
looked at me funny and turned away
I had my head on the desk all day.

I went home after school and put on
my bathrobe never did get used to
that humming silence   just sat
on the couch and stared out the picture
window or something   suddenly my
father walked in he was carrying
a pocketbook   and oh God
I knew.

Susan was eight in 1954 when
her mother, Doris, died of cancer.

My Mother Isn't Dead

I don't believe people die. They just go uptown.
To Bloomingdales.

—Andy Warhol

She's just shopping. On State Street in Chicago, at Marshall Field's, and above her on the building its ornate three-sided clock is stopped at 5 P.M. It is late November, 1954, cold enough so that she wears her good wool coat, the collar cinched up tight around her throat, and ankle-high galoshes with fake-fur tops. To keep her carefully waved hair from lake wind funneling between skyscrapers, she wears a sleek babushka knotted underneath her chin.

She's happy, pushing through the big crowds and brass revolving doors, heading straight for women's clothes where she leafs through racks of fitted suits with shoulder pads and piping. Soft gabardine swing coats. French-cuffed blouses with bone buttons. She fingers short-sleeved Orlon cardigans, finds everything she wants, but doesn't buy. She's there to see the spruce tree rise three stories in the center of the store, its golden swag and winking ladders of bright light. She stops to test Chanel and Shalimar from atomizers lined up on glass counters. Soon she'll leave to go someplace she can afford—Goldblatt's, Wieboldt's, Sears.

In this heaven, she's still thirty, her cheeks softly rouged, lips crimson, blotted to look natural, every shining hair still on her head in place. She stands on the corner. In one gloved hand, a shopping bag. In the other, ten cents for the bus to bring her home. Sharp wind makes her eyes tear. The light drops, pewter, mercury to lead.

At home, we've turned on the lamps. Supper's waiting on the stove. My face, pressed against the window's dark, looks back at me. Wet snow begins to fall.

At My Mother's Bedside

Bony hull and sunken wreckage, she sits
propped up by pillows, hands folded
like a splintered bow across her swollen stomach,
her thinned hair, a skullcap of dune grass.
I stand next to her, my throat, an ocean shell
filled up with sand, with everything
I don't know how to say. This room, a seine
float, wavery with limitation. Here, now,
life starts to blur, warps like fish underwater.
Outside, voices of my playmates yap joy
in early autumn. I am eight years old, learning
that no matter how much life is left for me,
its exquisite green glass will always be distorted—
death, a dark meniscus of salty water leaching in.

*Ruby was nine when her mother, Betty, died in
1981 from complications following surgery.*

The Rabbit Chase

It was one of the most gruesome and awesome things I'd ever seen in my life. I was ten years old. My mother had been dead for almost a year. My dad didn't know what to do. It was too much to ask—for a fifty-year-old man to take care of two girls, hold an important job, and look after such a big place—and then expect him not to drink. But he was doing his best, and for my sister and me, things were perfect just the way they were.

Until the day we discovered what we thought was our father's severed head stuffed in the glove box of his GMC pickup truck.

Our father farmed to keep sane, I'd once heard him tell my uncle. He lost money every year on the few acres he farmed, but he found comfort in tinkering with the old machinery and mastering the steep, prone-to-erosion hills that made up his dreamscape. We knew that if we ever lost him, it'd be out there. With our mother just gone we worried, constantly, that we would lose him.

Finally, on that spring day with the storm taking its time blowing in since morning, I knew we'd lost him. It was close to sundown and we hadn't seen Dad since lunch. We couldn't see or hear his tractor in the field. His radio in the barn was on, like it always was, broadcasting the Sunday afternoon baseball game. His truck was in the yard and there was a can of beer on the hood. When I picked up the beer and felt there was still half a can, we started to worry. Dad would never leave a beer lying around wasting like that.

He didn't answer our yells. We checked the house. It was a big house, too big for the three of us, but it wasn't supposed to be for just the three of us. We knew he wasn't in the house; he was never in the house. Maybe it reminded him too much of her. Probably he just preferred the outdoors, but I liked to think it had something to do with his missing her half as much as I did. It still smelled like her, the house. He still had most of her clothes hanging in their walk-in closet. Sometimes my sister and I would go in there and hug the empty dresses and pants and coats. He didn't like it when we did that. But he didn't get rid of the clothes for almost two years, until after his third date with the woman who would become our stepmother. He had let me keep her pillow. I wrapped it in plastic and stored it in a chest. I would take it out and smell her on the pillowcase, but it finally lost her smell and I got mad at her because it had lost her smell and I threw it out.

We couldn't find him anywhere. The windows on his truck were down and it was starting to sprinkle so I opened the doors to roll them up. When I opened the passenger side that's when we noticed the hairs sticking out of the glove box.

"What do you think it is?" my sister asked, reaching out her fingers to touch them. I grabbed her hand.

"No!" I snapped. "I don't like it. It looks like . . . "

"Like hair!" we screamed in unison. We left the truck door standing open and ran into the house. We locked all the doors. Neither of us said aloud what I suppose we both suspected immediately.

We probably would have calmed down and come to our senses if it hadn't been for a giant crash of glass and then, immediately, a smaller crash. We both screamed. We walked to the kitchen doorway and saw that the window above the sink had been broken, large shards of glass lay in the sink, on the counter, and on the floor. Also on the floor was a plate broken into small pieces. We would not walk into the room for fear that whatever was lurking outside, probably still below the kitchen window listening, would leap up and attack us.

I grabbed my sister's hand and ran, crouching to keep our heads below any windows, into our father's bathroom. We climbed into the shower and shut the frosted stall door. We were trembling and afraid to speak. We waited. At last, we each confirmed the other's fear—we both believed it was our father's head in the glove box, and whatever unknown evil had broken the window had also chopped off his head and was now after ours.

After many painful minutes, we tiptoed out and peeked into the kitchen. I decided to call our aunt, our mother's sister. We took the phone and ducked out of sight behind the sofa. I relayed our story, including the part about our father's head in the glove box, to my aunt. I thought that our aunt's clear lack of concern was because she lived in the city, a full hour away, and didn't want to drive all the way out to check on us.

I started by telling her that Dad's head was in the glove box. She chuckled. She was a big woman and she had a deep, soft, and hearty chuckle. When I told her about one of our strongest pieces of evidence—the unfinished can of beer—she exploded with laughter. But when I told her about the broken window and plate she did seem concerned. She tried to talk me through the possibilities. She said to call back if Dad wasn't home in an hour or if anything else strange happened. I crawled out from behind the sofa and hung up the phone.

"We're getting no help from her. She doesn't care about us. We're on our own," I informed my little sister.

"Why, what'd she say?"

I shook my head. "She said that a bird probably flew into the window and broke it."

My sister shook her head, "That'd be one heck of a big bird."

"That's what I told her, and she said that she'd seen wild turkeys fly into things before and that they have hard heads and so do big hawks or vultures."

"So it flew into the window, broke it, then flew up and hit that one plate on the wall and then flew back out?" my sister said in disbelief. "What about the hair sticking out of the glove box?"

I rolled my eyes and told her our aunt's theory, "Probably some of Dad's old dirty rags, she said, but I told her it was definitely hair. Then she said that it was most likely a rabbit's nest. Rabbits make nests in warm, dry places, she said."

"So the rabbit hopped in the truck, opened the glove box, made a nest, and then shut the glove box from the inside?" my sister asked.

We were determined to solve the mystery. We grabbed a baseball bat and a large glass of ice water. Our plan was that I would open the glove box, my sister would immediately dump the cold water on the head to stun it in case it was still alive, and then I would beat it to final death with the baseball bat. We both agreed that even if it was Dad's head, it was now possessed and must be destroyed. We were better off without it—and so was he.

We walked timidly out to the truck. The beer can was still on the hood, but the passenger door was shut.

"I could swear we left that door open when we took off," I said.

"Me too," my sister agreed.

I had the bat raised and walked over and picked up the can of beer from the hood, I gasped and dropped it.

"What?" my sister screamed.

I was trembling. "It's empty."

"Oh my god, oh my god, oh my god." My sister panted. "What do we do?"

We ran back into the house and went back to the shower and hid. Minutes later we heard the loud, retarded, familiar cough of Dad's old tractor—"Big Alice" he called it—shutting down. We ran to a window and looked out and we saw our father, head and all, climbing down from his tractor.

"Daddy!" we screamed and went running out of the house. He caught us in his arms but had a stern look on his face.

"What did you girls do?"

"Nothing, we swear," I said and told him how we'd heard the crash. He led the way into the house and kitchen.

Dad walked over to the sink and picked up a severely scuffed softball, looked up to the wall from where the plate had fallen, and smiled. "I was cutting the horse pasture with the big mower on the tractor," Dad said more to himself than to us. "I must have run over the ball and the blades hit it and projected it straight through the window and then up to the plate and then it rebounded back and landed in the sink."

We followed the imaginary path Dad routed through the window and up to the wall and back down into the sink. We all nodded and sighed, "Ohhh."

Reluctantly, we told our father that we'd called our aunt. He really wasn't happy about that because he would have to call her and explain. He didn't like having to explain things to her. Every conversation ended with "those girls need a mother."

"Why were you so scared?" Dad said.

Then we told him about the can of beer. He laughed. "When I came up from the field to mow the lawn, I noticed I'd left that beer there so I went over and drank it. Someone left my truck door open."

My sister and I looked at each other. Should we tell him?

"We saw some hairs sticking out of the glove box," my sister said. "They were gray and they looked like yours and we thought it was your head."

"Now how would my head get in there?" he asked. He didn't chuckle.

"We thought someone chopped it off and put it in there and that your body was driving the tractor without your head," my sister finished.

"Well, it's not my head," Dad said. We laughed and hugged him. "But the question is 'What is it?' Is it someone else's head?"

"Aunt Dee thinks it's a rabbit's nest," I said.

"Now how would a rabbit get in there and make a nest and shut the glove box?" Dad asked us. We giggled.

"She chuckled at us when we told her we thought it was your head in there," my sister told Dad.

"I suppose she did. She's a chuckler."

"And she laughed when we told her that we knew something bad had happened to you because we found half a can of beer," my sister went on. "We told her there was no way you'd leave that much beer in a can." I probably wouldn't have told him that part.

Dad nodded, "I'm sure she did get a good laugh out of that."

"And she said it was probably a wild turkey or vulture that broke the window," I added quickly.

"That woman thinks she knows everything about animals."

"That's exactly what we said. But we didn't think she was right so we were going to go open the glove box and find out for ourselves," I told him.

"Were you? But what if it's something alive in there?" he asked. We explained our plan. He nodded in genuine appreciation.

"Well, let's do it. Where's the bat? Grab another cup of ice water," he told us.

"It's nothing," I said. "We know we were being silly. We just got scared."

"How do you know unless we check?" he asked.

We approached the truck. Dad opened the passenger door and motioned for me. I had the bat; my sister the ice water. I nodded to Dad. He pushed the release button and jumped back as the glove box popped open. My sister blindly threw the ice water and ran from the truck. I got ready to swing. There was a large ball of fuzzy twine soaked with ice water. We laughed together.

"It does look like hair," Dad said, turning it over in his hands. It made us feel better.

It was almost dark and lightning heated up the sky. Our farm was on a large hill and was always hit hard by storms. When we first bought the place, when I was just five years old, there had been a large, hand-carved sign that read "The Windswept Farm" standing at the front of the long gravel drive. It had blown away. Only the posts sticking out of the ground remained; Dad hadn't gotten around to removing them yet.

"We better get inside," Dad said as he shut the truck door. We were headed back to the house and that's when I saw it—a large black rabbit streaking across the yard.

"Look!" I screamed and pointed. My dad and sister didn't see it. Then suddenly, the sky opened up and a huge bolt of lightning lit the entire yard and struck less than twenty feet from us. Thunder cracked and I felt my father's arms around us, pulling us to safety.

As the rabbit flew across the yard, headed for the open field, lightning struck it. It was like slow motion, in black and white. Like something out of a cartoon I'd seen. I don't know if it jumped or if the electric shock pulled it off the ground, but I saw its body twist and turn a foot, maybe more, above the earth. Then it fell flat to the ground.

"The rabbit! The lightning hit the rabbit," I cried. I tried to run over to it but Dad held me back.

"It's not safe now, we've got to get in," he yelled over the thunder and between the large, hard drops that were falling fast.

Inside I told him what I'd seen. He didn't say he didn't believe it, he just said it was hard to believe. He said he'd never been so close to lightning striking. He said he could feel the ground tremble beneath his feet. All I had felt was the rabbit's death. He went to take a shower and clean up for dinner and I slipped out the backdoor. The rain had stopped and the wet ground glistened yellow beneath the single yard light that had lost power during the storm but was buzzing itself back to life.

It was lying there, right where the bolt of lightning had left it. Its legs were stretched out in a running motion. It was on its side. Like I could go over and set it back up on all fours and it would take off, like those rabbits on sticks that greyhounds chase at the dog races. Except the entire underside of its belly was split open from its throat all the way back, exposing its dark pink innards that looked like a combination of mayonnaise, melted marshmallows, and pink food coloring. I didn't see any blood but it smelled like burnt meat. I bent over, to touch it, then I heard something and I jumped away. Before I could turn and run, I froze in terror as a coyote dashed in front of me, grabbed the dead rabbit in its teeth, and then trotted across the field and back down into the woods. The rabbit was already stiff in the coyote's clutch.

I started walking backwards to the house. I didn't want to turn my back on the coyote, and I was afraid he might be part of a pack. I tripped over a limb that the storm had ripped down. I landed hard on my tailbone. Then my stomach was dizzy and there was pain in my lower back, a dull throb. Then there was a warm, wet sensation between my legs. I hoped it was just the wet grass but I knew that wasn't it. I walked slowly back to the house and into the bathroom. I came out an hour later. My dad and sister were eating. I picked up the phone and crawled behind the sofa.

"Where you been? Who are you calling this late?" my dad asked.

"Aunt Dee."

"Haven't you bothered her enough today?"

"I want to apologize," I lied.

Aunt Dee answered.

"I think I got my period."

"How old are you?"

"Almost eleven."

"You're too young. That's not it. It's something else. Go tell your father." She started to say something else but I hung up.

I wasn't too young. That was "it." I never told my father. I'd take care of things on my own. I went into my bedroom and shut the door and took down all the pictures of my mother. My sister knocked and then cracked the door and stood there watching me.

"Why you taking those pictures of . . ."

"Mommy" was already a word that sounded strange when we said it aloud. So we'd just stopped saying it, gradually, and then altogether. I had just started to call her "Mom" before she died. It'd been almost a year. I wasn't even eleven yet. My aunt was right, I was too young, but that didn't matter.

"Did you see it?" my sister asked, excitedly, stepping inside my room and shutting the door behind us.

"See what?" but I knew what she was talking about.

"You know, the rabbit. Was it still out there? Is it dead? Will you show it to me?"

At least she believed me. She crawled into my bed and I held her.

"No," I said. "It was nothing. It was just my imagination."

RINA FERRARELLI

*Rina's mother, Antonietta Perfetti Ferrarelli, died
in 1949 of grief and tuberculosis when Rina was 10.*

The Day of the Funeral

No flames leap in the hearth,
the coals spent, the stone
swept clean. The people gone,
who pressed against the walls;
the relatives, who left her behind
to spare her. Alone, the child waits,
waits for someone to come,
watches from the shadows
the bright innocent light
cut across the empty bed,
carve new rooms out of the old ones,
silent and blank. She cannot go
past the threshold, imagine a life
without the light of her eyes,
without hands that move, feet.
Soon, she will leave for good
the home where she grew to the age
of reason, the age of grief. But now
she waits for someone to come,
inhabiting the still place
before the crossing, the light,
pure and colorless, and cold as marble.
A sigh, a white silent scream
gets lost in it. There is no room for pity.
Her life before that moment freezes,
begins to fade imperceptibly.
Everything looks the same, nothing

is the same. Her mother is gone.
Gone—a mouth, a window
through which the spirit leaves.

To My Mother

I hid in a dark corner, then,
and knees to chin
watched the daylight
slice through vacant rooms,
carve your face
in the hollow of window and door.

Later I made presence of absence,
and thought I was free.
But I couldn't listen to Chopin
or the sound of violins.

You're younger than I am, now,
and your children are the same age as mine.
And it still goes on.

Wind-scented children
chase each other through the yard,
run into the kitchen yelling,
tracking mud, fall asleep watching TV.
Ask questions
with answers too painful to give.

But you can't ever watch them
with favoring eyes, nor can you
bury your mouth on their necks
fresh as sun-dried linens.

Anne was five in 1957 when her mother,
Claire, died from a cerebral hemorrhage,
the day after giving birth to twins,
her sixth and seventh children.

The Black Box

I'm five-and-a-half years old, on a Saturday afternoon, kneeling in a dark corner facing the wall with all the drapes drawn and no lights on and I begin to go over and over in my head what I will miss most about not having a mother. The first thing I will miss about not having my mother is homemade oatmeal bread. Not just the taste and feel of the first warm and chewy slice melting in my mouth with butter, but the smell of it baking. A sweet smell with a touch of damp earth hidden in it like when you pick daisies and you pull too hard and they come out of the ground with their roots covered in dirt. The smell of oatmeal bread is a smell that says to me, as I come up the back stairs into the kitchen, she's home. No matter what Dad's up to tonight it's gonna be all right because she's home.

Then there is her voice that sometimes scolded us, sometimes screamed at the old washing machine when clothes got torn up in it. The steady calm voice that told and read the best stories. She always stopped to turn pages back so that I could look at pictures for the hundredth time. Go over every word and picture in the book again hoping for more time with her before she tucked me in and the lights went out. When I was sick, her soothing voice could cure me quicker than the St. Joseph's Baby Aspirin that I loved the taste of. Sometimes, I'd tell her I didn't feel good just to get the orange-flavored aspirin treat and the touch of her strong, cool hand on my cheek that could tell my temperature better than any thermometer. She could get me to stop crying by holding back my bangs with one hand while rubbing little circles around my back with the other while I pressed my wet face into the wide hip of her homemade madras skirt. Ever since Ma taught me about the word, "madras," I thought I smelled India whenever I buried my face in her skirt. The touch of her hand always spoke to me on Friday nights when Dad came home and it wasn't safe to talk. He never broke our code. Two slow pats on the back: stay in the kitchen and keep eating your fish and potatoes in silence. One quick pat on the back: leave the table fast and take the other kids with you. While all the time, he thought she was only leaning over to dish out more canned peas as he dished out stories about how hard a week he had on the road.

I think about this on a Saturday afternoon, kneeling in a dark corner where I am supposed to pray facing the wall in a room with all the drapes drawn and no lights on. I'm at my neighbor's house, trying to recite a string of ten Hail Marys with no rosary. But I keep hearing Dad's words to my older sisters Kata and Trudy, "Arlene, Matt, and Brad are going to the Du Pres' for the next three days because they are too young to see the coffin." I don't know what a coffin is, except that Dad said it was a black wood box. I knew it had something to do with Ma never coming home again and I knew what staying at the Du Pres' meant. My two brothers and I thought it was "Do Prays" because whenever Ma left us over there with old Mrs. Du Pres and her old daughter, we prayed all day.

On my twentieth Hail Mary, which is as high as I can count, when the pain in my knees feels like nails shooting through to attach me to the floor, I get a vision of Jesus on his cross and then I see Ma down at Coutu's Funeral Home. She's lying in a black box and I'm up here at Do Prays boxed in a black corner praying. And it's just like old Mrs. Do Pray says to us in her broken French accent: "You kids pray for your sins and maybe your mudder will make it to heaven, no?" Through my sinning wickedness, I have killed my mother. Matt and Brad helped out with all the choke cherry and apple fights and biting each other till Ma screamed and shook us. They helped, but as I think back to last year when I was four, I know what killed her.

She had caught me kissing Mark Flambé behind the oil tank. She was so mad she dragged me from the yard into the kitchen by my ponytail, then washed my mouth out with Fels Naptha soap to clean the sin out of me. That was one of the times I didn't like the sound of her voice that raged at me. "The Lord giveth," Ma said scrubbing the inside of my mouth with the bar of stinging soap, "and the Lord taketh away. Sweet Jesus, Mary and Joseph, please take these sinning ways away from my daughter. Arlene, you'll be the death of me yet," she said leaning over me. The heat of her breath in my ear felt like the summer wind blasting through the small sliding back windows of our Ford station wagon that make all the road noises blur into one roaring sound. I wished the bitter soap would wash the evil out of me, but while my ears rang hot with shame, I just kept thinking about those exciting kisses and that I couldn't wait to kiss Mark again. So God took Ma away instead.

Now Ma's dead and I'm at the Do Prays praying in a dark room, sleeping in a darker room in one bed with my two brothers. My younger brother is so mad or sad, I told Mrs. Do Pray he has just about stopped talking and started peeing the bed. But Mrs. Do Pray said she was ready for that, pulling back the white worn-out George Washington style bedspread, like the one Ma told me about on her and Dad's bed. I loved helping Ma tuck the soft balled-up cotton fabric under her pillows, pretending I was tucking my own baby into bed. When I got into Mrs. Do Pray's bed, a thin white sheet covered a thick rubber mattress pad making the bed smell like Brownie's Garage and Tire Center where I sometimes fell asleep waiting for Dad to catch up with Brownie over a coupla' Black Labels.

Mrs. Do Pray made us sleep in the bed with only our underwear on in case of an accident during the night. This morning, when we woke up with Matt's damp pee spots on our underpants and T-shirts, Mrs. Do Pray had a steaming hot bath waiting for us. We peeled off our smelly undies like we were told. Then she picked each one of us up under the arms and dropped all three of us into the same hot bath water. It burned my skin watermelon pink while my brothers' skin turned bright orange. I thought about the day Ma taught me two new words, "scald and blanch," as she dropped peaches into steaming water to remove the skin from the fruit before she canned it for the winter.

Inside my evil mind, the more I pray, I see that Mrs. Do Pray has left us alone. In my mind I see her walking down to Coutu's to visit Ma who I know is lying inside the black box and I suddenly remember that *American Bandstand* is on Saturday afternoon and I want to watch it. I don't care anymore about death and dark and sinning. I want light. I want to get up off my knees and move. If that makes for more sinning or even another death, I don't care right now because that's how bad I feel I need to move. "Hey Matt, I think Mrs. Do Pray is gone. Let's turn on the TV I think *American Bandstand* is on. Let's see." "O.K.," he says which are the only two words he seems to know how to say anymore. Even though he is younger than me, for his age Ma says he's smart with his hands like I am with words so I just know he can figure out how to turn on the Do Prays' brand new Zenith. When he turns it on, he blasts the volume and that wakes up my older brother Brad who has been asleep in the corner he kneels in. I tell Matt to leave it up loud because there is nobody around to hear Dick Clark who is smiling at us and welcoming back Chubby Checker.

The three of us start to twist in that dark living room like Chubby tells us to. We twist round and round and up and down, we twist like we did last summer, we twist like we did last year, we remember when things were really humming and we twist cause twisting time is here. We go round and round and up and down all over the living room. Then, Brad jumps on top of the plastic-covered couch and twirls round and round throwing bright colored crocheted cushions at Matt who bats at them with one of Mrs. Do Pray's walking canes. I keep on twisting right along with the girls on *American Bandstand*, copying their moves. Especially the dance steps of the blonde teen who I love to watch every week with her high-teased crown and a ponytail so long it twitches at the back of her knees when she does the shimmy.

We twist and shout and I have to have more than just the gray light coming in from the TV in the middle of a Saturday afternoon so I open the dark green velvet curtains with light green swirling roses cut into them. Then I go around and push back the white sheets from the huge living room windows because I see that the sun is out. I can't take another minute of this quick sick feeling in the dark that won't go away. The same quick sick feeling in my tummy when Dad throws me too far out into Spotted Lake during swimming lessons.

I have to come up fast for air. So after I push the sheets aside, I open the windows to the Saturday afternoon air while my brothers' twisting turns into a fist fight. But it doesn't last because as soon as Chubby is done singing, Elvis's "Hound Dog" record starts playing, which is their favorite because they love to hunt. That was the end of that dreary living room for them. Matt pushes me out of the way so that Brad can jump right out of the window. Then Brad reaches back in and pulls Matt and me out through the window and we tumble onto frozen brown grass but I don't feel the cold at all from all the twisting. And I don't believe it when I see the little black dotted holes of Mrs. Do Pray's old lady shoes planted in the dirt where I am looking down at my fancy footwork.

Handiwork

A chanting pot of coffee.
My fingers flute the edge
of an apple pie.

Potatoes fall
like carved ivory
from my hand.

Drawn to ceremony
ghosts of my clan
gather in afternoon sunlight

dusted with flour. I smile
sharing a thousand years of ritual
with my ancestors.

And sigh knowing this
is the closest I can come
to holding my mother's hand.

When Love Dissolves

We were watching *Heidi* on our black and white TV, when Dad came into the living room and said that Ma was not coming home from the hospital, that she had gone to be with the angels.

Dad was not alone as he spoke these words. I saw Ma standing right beside him, pressing a finger to her smiling lips. Sshhh! Don't disturb Dad, that finger said. She came towards me and held my hand.

Her touch so light and soft, Pop! We dissolved like bubbles blown from the foam in a Lux bath. We disappeared right into the television screen, flew through the tube to Heidi's secret forest and Ma said that's where she'd always be. Inside my beating heart that I could feel but never see in the cool green center of me.

Laurie was 10 when her mother, Blanche,
died in 1963 from metastatic breast cancer.

Mommy Haiku

I wake in the night
haunted by mommy longing
it's a bad case this time.

Why couldn't you have behaved like other dead people
and hung around me
like a friendly ghost?

Even in black and white
your beauty
dazzles me.

Living through cancer just like you didn't?
tell me what I should do
with this ironic blessing.

Sadness hangs off my shoulders
like a haunted shirt
that doesn't fit anymore.

In case you're wondering
I didn't listen to your desperate suggestion
to hit my head against the wall.

Show me a person who's never lost someone
and I can show you a person
who has never gnawed their own flesh.

Kneeling at the altar of memory
I remember I was abandoned
and force myself to stand and leave.

The same hands that
braided my brown hair
pulled it from the golden fire of the Chanukah candle.

I am practical enough
to prefer crying into a good bandana that can be wrung out
over a box of Kleenex.

My face is shaped like yours
so why is it
I didn't get your blond hair to frame it?

We named a boat after you, Mom
sailed it on the safe waters
of Crystal Lake.

Bare-breasted in the mirror
I can see what a looker you would have been
at age forty-seven.

God, keep my wits
while I leave them behind
for a while.

I'm done—can't think
about cancer anymore,
yours or mine.

Some daughters follow in their mothers' footsteps
in my case
it wasn't safe to track you too closely.

I missed the
molten strikes of teenage anger at you, Mom,
Saint Blanche.

I am filled with righteous anger
fury dogs me
it is hard to direct it at you.

After you died
I reached for chocolate when I longed for you
an addict was born.

I missed one complication
if you had lived
you wouldn't have approved of everything I did.

Lauren was a month from turning seven
when her mother, Irene Magyar,
died of lung cancer in the spring of 1991.

Cooled Wax Drippings

I don't remember
The sterile hospital smell.
Gone is the hope of that moment.
I can't see the sympathetic
Appearances on the doctors and nurses,
Sometimes replaced with smugness and jeering
Thrust at a six-year-old.
Gone are the footsteps
And cheerful greetings into
Other rooms,
But the hurtful, jealous sounds
Now
Echo down the hallways.

I still remember
The glimmering off-white walls,
The sunlight spraying in,
And pictures on the wall
My sister and I had painted
A little too late to be admired.

I remember my father
And the objective doctors gathered to
Witness final moments,
Her face the color of the walls,
The tubes that helped her to breathe;
Each breath,

Shallow and painful,
Revealed their uselessness.

My sister let go a
Scared whimper.
She was too young to be polite.
I remember the desperate expression
On my mother's face,
But most vividly, I remember
The tears collected on her face,
Like cooled wax drippings
Down the side of a candle.
She didn't look like mom,
As if
She was already gone.

Letter to an Irish Boy

To a distant figure stuck somewhere between memory and fantasy.
This hasn't happened in a while.
It must have hurt my father
to come into my room,
and see me sitting on the edge of my bed
mom's leather purse in my lap
and hear his favorite song from Andrew Lloyd Webber's
Requiem
as I quivered
with my hands where they had slid
to the end of my face
feeling my tears.

RUTH HARRIET JACOBS

Ruth was 10 when her mother,
Jane Gertrude Miller,
died from cancer in 1934.

Assistant

My mother liked baked custards
Lettuce sandwiches on whole wheat
And ginger ale ice cream floats.

When Mother was in cancer agony
And I was ten, my aunt took me
To buy ginger ale and ice cream.

We made a float with a lethal dose
"to put your mother to sleep.
You are a big girl" my aunt said.

Seventy years later I still dream
being the assistant angel of death.
I was not really a big enough girl.

Jen was nine in 1981 when her mother,
Patricia Cullerton Johnson, was killed in a
car accident with Jen's grandmother and
Jen's aunt, her mother's twin sister.

Hold It Under My Tongue

From the empty shelf to the windowpane, a bolted wire hangs, holding Mama's jeans that have dried like fingers wedged in mud. My tennis shoes are next to our one-legged washer. I bend down to pick them up by the laces, tie them together, throw them in my box. I lean into the wall like Mama did when I was small and came up to the zipper of her jeans. I hear Aunt Rita swear to the Blessed Virgin, Jesus, and all the saints. The pantry door bangs open. She pops in her head and says, "Your mother had no sense when it came to cleaning. She could never keep a damn thing neat."

I watch a line of dust settle and snake itself around a pile of mail below our door slot. Aunt Rita bends down to snatch up a handful of mail then swishes up her face when she bumps into Mama's stone sculpture of a woman with her mouth taped over by a piece of dish cloth.

"Swanee, take your box and go to the van. If I see you move from the front seat, there will be trouble," she says, picking up the arm and leg of Mama's broken statue.

A faint trace of garlic and ginger and Mama's Lily of the Valley perfume wiggles into my nose. Just before I close the door behind me, I can see Aunt Rita fidgeting into our chair. She drums her fingers on the arm while her legs bounce back and forth, kicking the coffee table and cracking the air in a thud-thud-thud.

Out in the parking lot, nothing has changed since Mama died two weeks ago. Everything is the same. The brown broken glass on the edge of the curb catches the sun. Parked cars with dented fenders, cracked mirrors, and loose tail pipes line both sides of our street. Old Pepsi pop cans, wrinkled potato chip bags, lost shoes, and oil spots in the parking lot—everything is the same. Everything smells familiar; Thursday's garbage is rotting in steel, city-issued trash cans.

Our apartment complex is old and brown brick with three floors high and six apartments across. It is shabby. But its shabbiness is mine, and was everything to Mama and me. It was our apartment, paid for each month on Mama's salary of welding iron trinkets on top of other iron trinkets, and mine as a part-time bagger at the supermarket.

I watch my street, searching for some signs of Mama. I don't see anything, except Mrs. McFadden call her dog. Her five kids hang on her until she pushes them away in a single whack. They all go flying in different directions, landing on the cement sidewalk or the grass or close to the barking jaws of the dog. Jack Harritigan and his gang of bullies play basketball by the dumpster.

I roll down the van windows, take out my Chicago Bulls T-shirt from my box, then wipe sweat from my forehead and upper lip. My hands pick through what I grabbed to bring to Aunt Rita's house where I will stay and walk on her soft brown carpet inside her two-story, brick house with its green garden hose and Weber grill. I have a rope belt, a pair of gym shorts, underwear, and gym shoes. The rest Aunt Rita said wasn't worth taking.

I touch everything and again my eyes get watery. I look in the side mirror and that's when I see it, a whirl heaving down the stairs. Aunt Rita's blue shirt flaps in the wind. She drags all Mama's things out to the dumpster. Her back hunches over from the weight of her swipe, as if she has tried to take everything at once, and throw it all away in one final swoop. Stalking up and down the stairs, sweating armpit stains, she slams the screen door shut. It bangs each time she goes in and out.

Mama's blue sweater, the one she slid on to wear to the movies, falls with the hanger still stiffened to shape. Her sewing machine that doctored up my Halloween costume plunges into brown stone dishes and both machine and dishes shatter to pieces. Lipsticks of red, pink and brown fall out of a box marked "personal" with a blue plastic handle and flip open their lids, oozing out colors. Black and purple belts, high heels, and beach sandals land in a thump. Necklaces with crystals crack and plastic, wood, and glass beads break and sprawl out in loud bangs on the steel floor of the dumpster.

Everything shatters, rips to pieces, and I can only mouth *Aunt Rita,*

God, Aunt Rita, and trip towards the sidewalk. My hands are shoved into my pockets, twisting the lint and clutching the spare change. Mrs. McFadden and the other neighbors, the ones who borrowed sugar from Mama, swapped food stamps, complained about the landlord and the rats are out gawking, as if this is a sideshow and I am the final act.

I want to say something but nothing comes out. Words get caught in my throat like cloth on barbwire.

u

Later, me and Aunt Rita ride back. We are stuffed in my uncle's work van where electrical wires, pliers, tapes, steel tools, and my cardboard box clink and clank when Aunt Rita crosses the tracks by the train station. This is where my neighborhood ends and hers begins. It is only a small seven-block stretch between the two, but the split scowls in my ear until my cousin Conrad screams, "What's for dinner? I'm hungry, Ma."

After dinner, I climb up the stairs to sleep in a bed where my feet stick out from thin yellow sheets and where each night since Mama died I struggle to rub away the nightmare from my head. I dream about my eyes. I dream that they are beaten and bruised. Everything is quiet but I hear and smell, touch. Mama whispers to me. Her voice surrounds me, covers over me, and sleeps on top of my ear. It is a beat-beat-beat of her words. *Swanee, Swan, can you see me? Can you see me?* I see nothing in front of me, nothing behind me, nothing to the side.

My arms brush back Aunt Rita's sheets. I try to stand up, but my legs cramp with a charley horse. I call out *Mama, Mama.* Her name comes from the back of my throat, rolls over my tongue, and echoes in my ear. I say *Mama* until the pain at my calf, throbbing like the size of a tiny boulder breaking apart, stops. I say *Mama* so the word won't disappear from the insides of my mouth.

When my muscle is back in place, I dig into my jean jacket pocket for smokes I swiped. There are two left. I shake one loose and glance out the window. There are stray branches from the willow tree resting on the back of the roof. The glare of the city light shines into my eyes and face. I turn away to light my first cigarette. I exhale like Mama, through my nose, and catch a shadow of myself outlined on the wall.

Then I climb out the window onto the roof. Roof to branch, branch to ground, I run the seven blocks through Aunt Rita's neighborhood. I pass tidy lawns, garbage cans next to the bungalow houses, and lights behind lace curtains. I walk the last half block back to our apartment and stop in front of the dumpster.

It shines underneath the security lights. It looks larger in the night. I open its metal lid then crawl into it. I rest my head on chicken bones, shredded lettuce, and a yellow blouse like it is Mama's lap. Mama's face floats in front of me, as if it belongs to some other girl. I touch my eyes, then, take back what I can. I dig my fingers through tin cans, sardine wrappers, and ripped curtains.

I stuff a photo of me and Mama eating a steak into my pocket. I remember what Mama told me when I wrapped fat from a cut of steak into a paper napkin. She caught my wrist and said, "Some of our family died with green mouths. But most of us lived." Then Mama shoved the steak fat in her mouth and pointed for me to do the same. I remember I held the gristle under my tongue before I swallowed.

Joanne was 15 months old when her mother,
Concetta Micciche Cannata, died in 1945.

Anthropology

The photos keep arriving in the mail.
Each sister sends one newly found
so I can see our mother when
she was young, then matronly,
standing on the hospital's lawn.
They do it to give me history,
to impress in my memory her
Kodachrome vitality, arranging
a chronology of missed years,
they dig for bones in cartons,
drawers and cardboard albums.
I reconstruct in black and white,
in color. She is almost solid, fleshed
with each new fragment: the infant
in her arms, the sisters' holding
her arms as she leaves the hospital.
Here her smile is less generous, more
tentative, the brows narrowed.
This must have been just after
the tumor blossomed, before
she lived from bottles and in charts.
Hair by muscle, I build the body
under which my girlhood lies,
below the carved stone. From beneath
red clay, anthropologists lift femur
and fibula, gently dust, arrange the ribs
of what lived, moved and was buried.

Her Blue Robe

I was never a bishop, but the world's
A dream we die in. I breathe

Into a blue robe, take day lilies
From a jar out of her room

To the pail in the yard. Who would
Believe the grass growing so quickly

Between the bricks, the purslane
Spreading like rash over the patio.

We're done with her dresses, hangers
And plastic bags, the trunk of yarn.

Stepping over collapsed boxes of shoes,
I carry the last collection of holy cards

To the yard and slaughter the saints
With scissors, that from these may grow

In full sight of her in pure stone,
The other life, continuing long.

Missing

It was a hard winter
of metal rivers and iron beds
certain disorder
uncertain sleep.
In the coming
and going of doctors,
how many saw her?
How many tried to imagine
tragedy like a train
roaring through a house
as a family sat eating
toast and jam.

Near-zero breath
after doctors tell the family
one is missing.
Her small daughters
look down at their dresses.
Their father makes fists.
Mother's in a building
snow on the roof and
bars on the windows.
Imagine a winter so hard
that no birds survive
and nothing moves in the ice.

ELIZABETH KERLIKOWSKE

*Elizabeth was three in 1954 when
her mother, Beverly, died in childbirth.*

Mother's Day

We force ourselves
we four   a family
to Muskegon to visit
Grandma. No one
likes her, my husband
least of all. His mother.
The hours are long
and loud with endless
jabber: q's without a's
the death count from
her high school annual.
At the lighthouse
I am strangely glad
my mother's dead
sure she was just
as I'd always heard:
perfect, undemanding
from under her stone
a lifetime of silence
filled with my poems.

Ramifications of Early Loss

I hug the nothing next to me
that snarls the covers in your place.
Yesterday's impression on the pillow
of your face turned in my direction
touches me in a way you cannot
not with lips, fingers or words.
I pitch my stone heart West this year
and follow its clattering to the mountains
far enough for now.
I will send my love in the weather
to storm over your state.
I will hallucinate your outline at my window
and cry for you, out to you
and be unmoved
for that is the nature of my childhood's disease:
I love you both, your presence
but your absence most.

Size 12

On the cusp of womanhood
I stood alone
my grandparents and sister gone to town
I stood alone a lot
in my grandmother's nightie
worn flannel like ghost arms
draped around my shoulders
sifting across my knees
in the bedroom mirror
where I lived then

covered with white flannel
and a field of fading cornflowers
like the cornflowers and chicory
scraping our shins in the dry gulleys
freckles cross my nose
like the gravel sprayed up
in the wake of the hooligans' pickup trucks
my hair was loose that day from
swimming   no time to braid
no grandmother home to pull the pieces tight
I heard my mother's ball gowns
rustling in the dress-up drawer
black silk and plaid taffeta
a heavy bittersweet sateen
like a movie theater curtain
all my sister and I knew of her
photographs and the feel of the clothes
I discovered myself in the embrace
of the strapless white chiffon
and in the oracle of the mirror
where her wistful eyes peered back
like planets in the constellation of my face
inside the restless dress
in the presence of flannel
my mother and I met

Holiday

My mother grew in the center of the family circle
a Christmas tree
a memory poky and sharp.
When I reached for it
I cried.

Every Christmas held a funeral
of ornaments.
I had my favorites
watching them be born
from tissued boxes once a year:
red and red and red.

Celluloid balls
the hulls of joy.
Clamp-on birds of paradise
their tails long gone
so hollow they had to be arranged
facing away from the trunk.
Gilt and cotton stuck to me.
Even sleeves didn't help.
My arms came out
with a lasting rash.

The angel hung below the star
which fit on a coiled spring
a hole in its heart for the light.
This was the hardest part.
My grandmother needed a ladder.

Each crowning of that tree
was a gardenia lovingly arranged
was a French braid
was a knit hat tied tight
by a mother who lost her child
to the elements anyway.

Laid to rest first
the bright tin star
came out last, the beautiful
compelling afterbirth that
decked the tree with sorrow.

Grandpa went then to get more wood.
My sister clung to Gran who wept.
I memorized the carpet fibers.
It felt wrong to want
the bright caskets of presents.

MIRIAM KESSLER

Miriam was seven in 1931 when her mother,
Sophie Harriet Langman Barkus, died of cancer.

Letter to Mother

I have been waiting for you to come back.
No one told me you were dead.
It's a game they play
to keep the kids from being sad.

I know you sleep beneath the azaleas.
But we had irises every year
every bit as good as your azaleas.
The women from the sisterhood
paid for a memorial plaque
and I say the **Kaddish**
as a loving daughter should.
In your name I made a son,
Stephen, for your name, Surila,
and the three granddaughters
have waist-length hair.

Yis ke dol
vi yis ke dosh
the rabbi sang.
They let the ropes grow slack
around the plain pine box
and mailed you off to God.

Kathryn was 16 in 1974 when her mother,
Eleanor Mae Smith, died from a
prescription narcotic drug overdose.

Tachycardia

1

The black medical bag
was inside the white Dodge.
Dr. Thompson eased his car
into our driveway.
The car was meager for a doctor.
I imagined the bumpers
painted black
to match
his black plastic glasses.
But his eyes gleamed
behind the glare of glass
a menacing frown.
I could see myself reflected.
I should be ashamed, he said,
for leaving my mother, Eleanor,
alone.

2

The sun shown through the
pink curtains in her bedroom.
I smelled the paint bake
on the window sill.
I smelled the illness
of her terrible inaccessible stillness

and everything changed.
I had to stand outside
on the driveway
to keep myself complete.

3

These were episodes
of foreboding.
My mother called them
her attacks.
Her heart
bruised her from the inside.

4

She wore her red robe
like a shroud
caked blood pasted permanently
over thumping skin.
I wanted to rip it
off her body
and burn it.
Maybe the smoke would
personify her spirit.

5

I had stood inside her
bedroom vault before
in a sun shower
a breeze billowed the curtains
and whispered to me
about benevolence and beauty
outside
before I knew the routine
of her need.

6

It started in the street
shopping or driving
pains rose in her heart.
Fright frantically pumped
through veins
and back again.
Her fear filtered through
a nervous organ.

7

She was disabled
by dread
and suffered in her bed
with sips of whiskey
until the neighbors came
a nurse, Naomi,
a friend, Jean.
The doctor in his white Dodge
who blamed me for
inflaming her heart.
He carried the black medical bag
into the house
like a chalice
his face full of malice.

8

He put the black bag
on the white night table.
I could see his face relax
when he sat on the bed
and held her wrist
like a limp snake.
The pulse of her life
was out of control.

9

I had seen the racing
in a rage, a gauge,
the deep furrows between
her eyes
after all the lies I told
to stay safe.
The attacks were like
disassociated pain.
I imagined ripping the muscle
out of her chest,
squeezing until blood popped
on her red robe.
Then she would be still
and the panic in me
would sleep.

10

The doctor had other plans.
Hands for calming
or embalming.
His white hand against the black bag.
He dipped inside
and rummaged
his arm caught in the black muck.

11

It was not the first time
I had seen a
long syringe
and tourniquet.
My brother Tim used a belt or
the little ring my hand formed.
Dr. Thompson held a delicate
glass bottle

so tiny I might covet it
a vase
for dollhouse flowers.
The needle was clean, pristine
broken fresh from
a white wrapper.
Tim had one needle
that needed to be cooked
along with the heroin.

12

The stab of glimmer
was more intimate than
her kiss, a feeling
remiss.
But the silver needle slid easily
deliciously
into the green vein.
The red dot on her white skin
a drop on top of a hole
a spot to stretch and enter in
where I could begin to feel
the velvety warmth of her liquid life.
I grew smaller staring at the sight.
Dr. Thompson withdrew a patch of
gauze to pat the wound.
The leaves crackled
the curtain blew
in the warm red wind.
A desolate sound
I could not rescind.

13

The furrows in her face relaxed
her azure eyes grew vacant.

But a smile appeared
so deeply self-accepting
it radiated reverence
for the people and
the colors and
the movement in her room.

14

Suddenly I was summoned
to her bedside where
she rested a limp hand
on my thigh
her dead eyes unconnected to her smile
she murmured words of love
to her lovely daughter poised
with sun yellow hair
while a trail of boys
outside
tracked her beauty.

15

After the shot
Eleanor praised
the objects and the people in her room.
It was a love affair with matter
that was not possible
before the shot.

16

Every nerve ending was numbed
in ecstasy she floated through
all the encumbering discomforts
even the pressure of the sheets on her skin
was not taken in
the chafing weight of crossed legs

lifted like goose down
and the autumn breeze crested down.

17

The nurse, the neighbor, and the doctor
nodded tacitly
slinked
out of the room and
whispered like wind shears.
I had heard it all already. I
only imagined myself in the room
in third person, watching
as her attendants processed
outside.

18

Dr. Thompson in his black coat
had renewed wrath. He thought his
disturbance
was about me.
The white Dodge could have been a hearse
or his horse.
I detested him and
the Northern New Jersey sky
without understanding why.
It faded like my mother's eyes.

19

The neighbor was a savior.
Beautiful Jesus.
She had loved me without fading.
The nurse was present but gray
from chain-smoking Pall Malls.
Her spirit was made visible in smoke.
She's resting now, Naomi said and

left with my beloved Jean.
They chatted about their normal life
without children.

20

My mother's bedroom window panes
framed
the orange sunset
and broke the images of reality
outside
as if beauty was not continuous.
I saw the shade pulls like nooses
through the cut pictures.
She would want them drawn by dusk, but
what did she know of ritual in the switch between
calamity and calm?

21

Later on
her heart may have pounded
for the morphine
instead of love.

22

When she recovered and
the drug still held
they all went out to dinner.
The nurse, the neighbor, and
the husbands.
My father drank a
Smirnoff vodka martini
on the rocks
with an olive.
Nurse Naomi had a gin and tonic and
neighbor Jean drank gin straight up.

My mother had a Manhattan, the
men drank beer.
I knew this from the
card and clam parties, the
neighborhood holidays, the
wet celebrations.
They tried to get something from
each other
in secret
even while their words broke down
to sounds
I could not understand.

23

It was frantic
distraction
from their lives, perhaps, or
in the end, me.
That was my reaction.
For in the end I
could not engage them
their loud laughter and largess
as if they were enraptured with
themselves.

24

They all smoked except for
Eleanor.
How could they know about the
horrors
of their habits?
What tore away their plantings
that grew like flowers in
the late suburban sun
on this day or any other?

25

Later, Eleanor was radiant with alcohol
The soft red flush of warmth
was promiscuous joy.
Her altered attitude
the social swelling of benevolence.
My father's lap became
a spot on the map among
seductions
abbreviated connections that were
elated engagements
of love.

26

A slice of street lamp
lit their form
in the family room.
Later he would carry her, limp
along the floor, her body crossing his
but not as lucid as when she leaned into his lap
and waved goodnight to me
or goodbye.
Then she was upright in the shadow
of his flesh
and mine
for the last time.

27

The final disturbance disconnected me
like broken pictures.
The scene was like a movie
and I watched
unmoved:
Eleanor woke late in the black November fog
she crawled out

along the gold rug
through her own pools of rejected drugs
and her voice carried the urgency
of airborne illness.
I saw her red robe against the gold rug,
her long brown hair
tinseled fluff upon the floor.
She called, reached out through fog
I imagined she saw herself escaping
until Dr. Thompson came with
the black medical bag
and the white Dodge was in the black driveway.

28

Eleanor was comatose
for weeks
until Thanksgiving
when her heart stopped
in a snarl of tubes
and the furrows in her brow
relaxed
upon her white skin.

29

She was closely guarded: I was her
calm strong daughter
because I closed my door against the
reach of my mother's need
even as she called
I stood inside a sanctuary safely shelled against the
loss of self
for another twenty-nine years.

Jean's mother, Maude, died from heart problems
in 1938 when Jean was nine and a half.

I Remember, or Do I?

I recently met with three other women my age. We're in our seventies now, but we all went to kindergarten in the same small town. After lunch we gathered around a table in the local museum to chase memories through the pictures we brought.

After husbands, children, and grandchildren had all been duly admired, divorces enumerated, and two widows had received sympathy, Betty produced a pile of stiff, eight-by-ten class pictures, worn around the edges. She explained her ninety-year-old mother had recently died and the pictures had been found in the attic.

When I was young—I'm talking the 1930s Depression era—there were no individual "school pictures" as we know them today. People simply couldn't afford them. Instead each room, which contained two grades, assembled in the gym in turn and each had a class picture taken. If your family could afford it, they bought one. Since my mother was terminally ill, requiring constant medical care, we couldn't.

I looked at myself in kindergarten. I was small so I had been seated in the front row. I wore a dress and though the picture was black and white, I remembered my sweater was yellow and had two small brown yarn dollies dangling from brown yarn attached in the center for decoration. I'd watched my ill mother lovingly knit that sweater in spite of her heart trouble. My face was round and happy; my fair hair cut short at the ears with bangs covering my forehead.

I was not in the first- and second-grade pictures. I must have been absent those days.

"Look at me," said Margaret. "I'm frowning in kindergarten and still frowning in next year's picture. Wearing the same outfit, too. You'd have thought I'd could have changed my expression, and I know I had more than one dress."

Frona laughed. "I remember thinking you were rich, so you must have had more than one."

"Well, we *weren't* rich, but Grandpa lived next door and he had a huge garden and Grandma had chickens so we always ate well." Margaret frowned again, trying to remember back to those days. "My father worked for the post office so he always had a paycheck. Lots of fathers didn't."

I picked up the third- and fourth-grade picture. In this photo I am still positioned in the front row, but now I am a nine-year-old waif in round ugly glasses and a very thin summer dress. Since everyone else is wearing winter clothes, I look like a child uncared for. Again I have on a sweater, but I don't recall its color. It, too, is hand knit, but it's too small for me. My straight hair is crookedly parted on the side and barely held in place with a barrette. Obviously, I'd combed it myself.

It is my face, though, that stuns me. I remember my early childhood as one in which I was loved and cherished and well cared for, in spite of the Depression and my mother's illness. But my empty face shows no hope, no happiness, and no expectations. Clearly I've heard of impending disaster too many times and I'm teetering precariously.

In the thirties, if you had severe heart problems, the most you could hope for was to be kept comfortable until you died. In preparation, when I was five, my mother started telling me she would die before I grew up. She repeated this frequently with assurances that Daddy would either take me out to the Canadian prairies where his family lived, or her sister, my Aunt Olive, would take me home to Montreal to be her little girl. Each time she ended her word pictures with "Always kiss me goodbye when you go out. Some day when you come back I won't be here."

I accepted this as a fact of life, along with breathing, and I don't re-member worrying a whole lot about it. Children are resilient. But in building defenses, we create layers of eiderdown to cushion against rock-slides. With each assault we add another layer. So, I'd always remembered those days before my mother died as happy ones.

This small face was beyond worry, though. It had reached despair. I had a loving mother whose illness was too overpowering to allow her to deal with the daily problems of a young daughter. So this face had no one to depend upon but herself. And my carefully blank expression said that burden was too much.

With the picture in my hand, I sat bewildered. Then I became angry. How could I have fooled myself this way? For sixty years I'd remembered a happy childhood I plainly had not had. And why did no one help me?

Perhaps someone had. In 1938 the summer was hot and my mother was confined to bed as she'd been for over a year. Aunt Olive came from Montreal for a week's stay. My mother died, unexpectedly, on the second day. Was it just a coincidence she died while her sister was there, to see how lost I was, and to take me safely with her before my sad father could formulate other plans?

A heart pill too many or one not taken at all would have done it. I'll never know and I'll always wonder. And yes, I kissed her before I went out to play, and as she had predicted, she was "gone" when I came back.

When I got home after our get-together, I searched until I found the class picture taken my first year in Montreal. I am still in the front row, wearing a Catholic school uniform and the face that stares back at me is fuller now, and the hair is neat. The eyes are not haunted and this face shows a child who has reached safety. This part of my childhood is as I remembered it.

*Susan's mother, Florence "Sis" O'Donnell, died
of a brain tumor in 1965 when Susan was 14.*

World View

I had always loved the world map,
whose pastel shapes lent me endless possibilities.
I'd travel first to the boot of Italy,
I had decided in fourth grade.

When my mother died,
my world so filled with sorrow,
there was no room for hope.

And I wholly accepted
that those pastel shapes
belonged to someone else.

Tekla was 13 when her mother, Marion Kolk
Dennison, died by suicide in 1956, four years after
the death of Tekla's father. She then became the
ward of her 23-year-old sister, a single mother.

Lessons My Mother Never Knew She Taught Me

My mother, Marion Kolk Dennison, often greeted me after school performing a Russian Cossack dance across our red brick linoleum floor.
From a squatting position with her arms crossed over her full breasts and
a butcher knife secured between her teeth, she'd kick her legs out from
under her blue plaid housedress.

Each time it was the same. When she'd finished kicking across the
room to where I was standing, my mother would jump up, take the knife
from her mouth, and let out a glass-shattering laugh. Then she'd put on
the recording of Benny Goodman's 1938 concert at Carnegie Hall and
shimmy while stepping around me in a circle. Each time, I swore I'd never
join her in this ritual. But I always did. Eventually we'd jitterbug to our favorite Goodman piece, "Sing Sing Sing," and then collapse onto the couch,
out of breath and laughing.

My mother's daily attempts to keep her body trim by butt-walking
across the same linoleum floor to the rhythms of the Big Bands were
sabotaged by consuming lemon meringue pies she'd make in ten-inch
cast iron skillets. Lemon meringue was my brother's favorite pie and she
would use any excuse to bake him one—birthdays, Christmas, Thanksgiving, graduation, baseball victories, baseball losses.

Though my mother was devoted to lemon meringue pies, dancing,
and Benny Goodman, housekeeping was her passion. With her head
wrapped in a white terry cloth turban and armed with dust cloths, mops,
Bon Ami and vinegar, she'd attack the house, singing, "Life is just a bowl
of cherries. Don't take it serious. It's too mysterious. So live and laugh
at it all."

Despite my mother's pursuit of cleanliness, neighborhood children were never turned away from our door. Instead each day after school, my friends and I gathered around the TV to watch *The Mickey Mouse Club*. In winter, while my friends, as many as ten, and I huddled around the TV in our living room, my mother made cocoa in a huge saucepan and scooped it into cups using a soup ladle. She'd serve each of us a steaming cupful topped with marshmallows, but never scolded when the cocoa missed our mouths and landed on the floor.

My mother was determined to make me a dancer with the New York City Ballet Company in spite of my resolve to be "one of the boys." From the time I was five years old until her death, she had me taking dancing lessons and performing in yearly spring recitals. As part of her determination, my mother also enrolled me in my school's ballroom dance class. My partner Gary and I had other ideas. He wanted to play golf and I wanted to play baseball, so we often skipped dance class, which became evident during our performance at the end of the year. Though I looked the part of a ballroom dancer in a lavender taffeta dress cinched at the waist by a large sash and bow my mother made for me, I'm sure the Viennese waltz was not meant to be danced the way Gary and I did it. After that performance, my mother gave in and let me get on with being a real teenager dancing the jitterbug with my best friend Kay at the Friday night sock hops in the school gym while Gary and the guys watched from the sidelines.

My mother also resolved that I would be well rounded and far removed from my father's world of baseball, the railroad that employed him, and the town bars. She created an environment filled with classical music and wonderful books. She scrimped to save enough money to take me to the opera. My first was *Rigoletto*. I was seven years old, and I cried when I could not stay to see it again as we could at the movies in those days.

As one of nineteen children and like many women of her generation, my mother never went beyond the eighth grade in school. Yet, her lack of education did not intimidate her. She went to the library every week, borrowed seven books and read one a night. These were books like *Anna Karenina* and *The House of Seven Gables*. She even changed the name of our cat to Yahooty when a feline in a novel had captured her affection.

Through Benny Goodman, books, ballet, opera, and, yes, she even gave in to baseball, my mother encouraged me to explore the world and its options. I don't recall her ever saying that gender would obstruct any goal I wanted to achieve. Yet she'd often let me know "sacrifice is part of living." My mother was developing my self-esteem by allowing me to be a person within my own right, and to choose my own destiny.

Today, I laugh at the brown lace-up Oxford shoes my mother insisted I wear "to protect your feet for ballet." I called them my Red Cross shoes. My friends called them barges, a difficult image to live with in the 1950s when all the other girls wore saddle shoes or bucks. I'm convinced that those shoes were not only protection for my feet, but served as another lesson: My mother wanted to discourage my need to be like everyone else and encourage independent thought and action.

One August day in 1956, when I was almost thirteen, I vented all my pubescent hostility on my mother over some now-forgotten conflict between us. I screamed, "I hate you. You're crazy." Then I ran from the house slamming the door behind me. My mother committed suicide the next day. She had just celebrated her forty-first birthday and had been a widow for four years.

Gone were the nights sitting in bed with her reading library books, our backs propped against pillows supported by a brown metal headboard. Gone were the magical moments jitterbugging to Benny Goodman. Gone were the lemon meringue pies. Gone was the optimism in her singing, "Life is just a bowl of cherries."

While fighting the guilt brought on by my last words, "I hate you. You're crazy," I was also angry with her for leaving me. As I grew older, however, the lessons I learned from my mother during her short life overshadowed that anger and guilt. Her messages to me also became clear: she wanted me to have more than she did. I also discovered she suffered from depression which resulted in an emotional death. Even though her suicide seemed to contradict her ambitions and view of what could be, her lessons motivated me to search for excellence and influenced the direction I traveled in both my career and personal life. So as I pondered her life and actions, love and admiration for my mother replaced my anger and grief, and I felt sorry for the world that would never know her as I did.

For me there was no better way to honor my mother than to achieve what she never had the chance to do herself. So I'm thankful that the happy memories and lessons of my mother now outweigh the one of the sheriff lowering her body from a basement rafter.

The day I decided not to become a ballerina was a month after my mother's suicide. I was living with my sister, Alyce, who was my guardian, and I had just turned thirteen. I sat in a swing on the school playground, a half-mile from the home I had shared with my mother. I glided back and forth in the swing dragging my feet in the sand trying to make sense of her death. On that day the words she had dished up, along with the morning doses of oatmeal, echoed in my ears: "Education will be your ticket out of poverty. You can be anything you want with the right education." In that schoolyard, I decided to go to college, and I eventually pursued an unconventional career for a woman.

My mother's words inspired me to face each day with energy and curiosity, and to accept life's challenges as new adventures. Without that encouragement, how would I have had the fortitude to embark on a male-dominated career in corrections without fear? Her words, "You can be anything you want to be," gave me the determination to ignore the mores established for women of my generation and become the warden of a maximum security prison for men outside of Detroit.

Yet my career choice did not overshadow my mother's other lessons. I am a voracious reader, and I danced until arthritis made it impossible. I still go to the opera and clean house to Benny Goodman's 1938 Carnegie Hall recording. I treat each child I meet as a gift, as my mother did, and spend much of my retirement working to better the world for our children.

I am grateful for my mother's lessons of encouragement, optimism, and generous love, and for protecting my feet, which allowed me to walk the many miles I did through the prison for six years making daily rounds as a warden. The end was not what she envisioned for me or my feet, but I think she would respect the direction I chose to travel. Whatever the environment, I fulfilled her vision for me of becoming an independent and nontraditional woman—someone I am sure she also wanted to be. I feel my mother would not be disappointed in the fact that I traded in a fanciful ballet setting for razor ribbon, gun towers, and M-14 automatic rifles. Somehow, I think she would understand.

Laura was 16 when her mother, Sue,
died from pneumonia in 1971.

After

For years, her silk dresses hung in my closet
beside my T-shirts and jeans,
her clothes several sizes smaller than mine.
They lost her *My Sin* scent but kept her shape.

Her death, a month after I turned sixteen,
made me the enemy of an empty room.
For several weeks "Mom!" echoed
like a canyon. She didn't hear about

the rubber cheeseburger I ate for lunch,
or why I got thrown out of the school library
or why I needed her to tell me my hair was a mess
and ask me, *is that what you're wearing?*

Living Room

Lawn chairs and
a three dollar desk were
the furnishings we used after
my mother died.

We moved across the country
leaving
everything behind,
her body, her soul,
her living room.

We started over,
broken pieces of a shell,
using strangers' castoffs,
the impact of her
death hidden behind
newly collected artifacts.

Shannon was 15 in 1985 when her
mother died as a result of blood clots.

Hurt

She asked me where you were,
Though it seemed she already knew.
She said she felt your presence
Before she ever saw my face,
That you shouted, loud and clear.
She told me you are always with me,
That you ask for my forgiveness;
That you weren't ready for your children,
And your world turned upside down.
She said you offered me a shiny, new
Red wagon: a symbol of a lost childhood
That you cannot now replace.
I cried.

There is more peace than before,
Yet, I still remember
My visit to your deathbed,
Those final words you spoke to me:
"This is your fault," you said.
I came to tell you that I loved you.
Why didn't you let me?
"I did nothing to you," I said.
You turned your face away.

Christine Bollerud (on her mother's lap)
*This is the only picture I have with my mother. I was perhaps two years old in this
picture, four when she died.*

Jeanne Bryner (right)
The temple of memory is lit with simple candles.

Janet Buck
Janet and her mother at Janet's birthday party.

Susan Elbe
Susan and her mother, summer 1950.

Rina Ferrarelli
Rina with her mother and Fido in Italy.

Laurie Gass
Mom and me on post-graduate day.

94 ·

Ruth Harriet Jacobs

Ruth Harriet Jacobs and her mother, Jane Gertrude Miller.

Elizabeth Kerlikowske

Elizabeth is taught early to reach for what she wants.

Susan O'Donnell Mahan
*Susan, between her parents and with her sisters, is a flower girl at her
Aunt Mary's wedding.*

Tekla Dennison Miller
Easter Sunday, April 1956.

Laura Moe

I was thirteen in this picture. It was the age when I usually frowned or rolled my eyes at everything my mother said and did.

Ann O'Fallon
Ann, her mom and baby sister, Maureen.

Melissa Palmer
Me and my mom being cool as usual.

Diane Payne (standing)
It felt good to laugh, really laugh, during Connie's fifteenth birthday.

Cindy Pinkston
Cindy and her mom.

Rachel Pray
My mother, my brother, and me, Iceland, 1970.

Marjorie Snodgrass
Marjorie, age six years, with mother and brother, Robert, summer 1935.

Laurie Summer
Laurie at 14 months with her grandfather, father, and mother, Alice.

Zahava Zofia Sweet
Me and my mother on a stroll.

Alison Townsend

*Alison with her mother, Mary Doak Townsend, six weeks before Mary died,
November 1962.*

Margaret Vaillancourt
Margaret (Vicki) age one, sits on the lap of her mother holding a dollie with her sister, Debbie.

Patti Wahlberg
My mother and me about 46 years ago—I guess I'd rather be playing.

Anna M. Warrock
Anna, on her mother's right, and her sister Natalie show off their yellow mother-daughter dresses.

Kourtney Wheeler
Mom, my brother Justin, and me.

Allison Whittenberg

Some members of the Whittenberg family: Mother (Faye), Daddy (Luther), older brother (Rodney) and sister (Allison). My younger sister Beverly is missing from this photo.

Arlene Zide
Mommy, Bube, Grandpa, and me in the Bronx.

114 ·-

ANN MURPHY O'FALLON

Ann was nine when her mother, Ethel Marie
Koelzer, died from breast cancer in 1956.

Lilacs

We run home, new sneaker soles squeaking against hard sidewalk. The lilacs' perfume fills our lungs as we hurry past the city park, the metal chains on the swings clang softly as we go by. Four of us try to fit on the sidewalk as we're running, but we can't work it out right. My little sister struggles to keep up. I go as fast as I can to stay close to the boys and not screw up by stepping on a crack. It could break my mother's back, and she already has enough problems. My big sister is not with us. Where is she, did they call her, too? The movie had just started when Mr. Harriman found us sitting in the dark and said, "You Murphy kids are supposed to go home."

The priest had come before supper that night to give my mother Extreme Unction, the Last Sacrament. We had to dress up for him and I didn't want to. I pulled off my jeans and yanked the only dress that fit me off its hanger. I wanted to ask my big sister, who's thirteen, what was going on. Mary, the oldest of us kids, thought I was a twerp. "It's because she is dying, don't you know anything?" she snapped, closing the door to her room so fast that the May Altar to the Blessed Virgin jumped.

It isn't dark yet and the lilac scent is warm and comfortingly familiar as we run. None of us is talking much, just wondering where Mary is and if we are supposed to be finding her.

We were told to go to the movies, but she must have gone to the OK Cafe to hang out with her friends because she wouldn't want to be caught dead with the rest of us.

We crash through the back screen door as usual, a small herd of children. The kitchen lights are on, and my dad and aunt are standing by the table, faces broken with tears. Shocked, I wait just inside the door, the screen prickling at my long thick braids. I catch my breath while I take in the scene. I've never seen grown-ups cry before. Nothing in my life helps me prepare for this moment, and try as I might, I can't make sense of it. My nine-year-old mind scrambles to find a story I can live with. Then it comes, and I know in my heart it is true. I can see the fleeting outline of beautiful winged angels hovering near the window. It's a miracle. A miracle happened while we were gone! Nothing else could possibly make my dad and no-nonsense aunt cry. I ask, "Is she cured?"

No one says anything back to me. Maybe I didn't talk loud enough or maybe the question never left my head. The bedroom fixed up for my mom is right next to the kitchen. I know my mom has been sick because she wears a back brace. I know she had her breasts removed and wears falsies in her bra. Sister Angela Ann asked me if it was okay for our class to pray for her each day at school. We'd never prayed for anyone I knew before, just for the poor pagan babies in Africa, and I wondered why she asked me. My mom is always there when I come home from school, sitting in her chair reading or watching TV. And she is always at the table when we eat supper, so how sick can she be?

I follow everyone into the bedroom, still hopeful. She is there, in her bed, looking like herself, but way too still, still in a way I know is not okay.

Part of me understands now that Mr. Allen, the undertaker, will be coming for her soon. I used to play with his niece, Georgia, and we scared ourselves silly knowing dead bodies were on his back porch. I don't want to think of her spending the night at Mr. Allen's house rather than here, at our house, resting in her own bed. I kiss my mom by the eyebrow closest to me and touch her soft wavy hair. The firmness of her forehead startles me and I move far away, until my back hits the wall. A golden globe of inexpressible sorrow moves north from my heart and plants itself firmly in the soft tissues of my throat.

There we stand, the remains of my family. My father pulls over a chair and stretches the telephone cord to reach where he sits. He opens his address book and starts making calls saying the same thing over and over. It's like the phone has an echo, "Ethel died tonight," "Ethel died tonight," "Ethel died tonight." Finally he can't do it anymore and he puts the telephone away. He reaches in his pocket and pulls out his worn black rosary. There is a drawer beside him loaded with rosaries and he hands one to each of us. Then he kneels by the bed like he does every night to say his prayers. We all kneel, too, elbows on mom's bed, fingers gripping the colored beads. My dad leads, but his voice keeps breaking up, so my aunt has to start the Hail Marys and name which mystery we're on. After the last Hail Mary of the last Sorrowful Mystery, my aunt says my little sister and I can sleep in her bed tonight. We never sleep anywhere but in our own beds, so the promise carries us as we go upstairs and put on our pajamas. My aunt's room is the farthest from the front door, so I don't hear when Mr. Allen comes. And I don't hear him when he leaves.

The next morning I wake up early in Aunt Frances's soft double bed. The sun is shining in her windows and a fresh Iowa breeze blows through the curtains and over the two of us. The bells at St. Mary's Church ring every fifteen minutes so the whole town knows what time it is. There is a special ring for each quarter hour. As I lay there with my still sleeping sister the bells start their call. I recognize the pattern, the bells are tolling, and then I begin to count, their haunting cadence rolling out across the prairie. With the last ring everyone will know what happened at our house last night. It takes a long time. Forty-six, forty-seven, forty-eight, and I can't pretend anymore it isn't true.

Nancy was eight when her mother, Mamie
Alberta Moses Seale, died from a stroke in 1944.

Orange-Red Indian Paintbrushes

for Mamie Alberta Moses Seale 1901–1944

Three quarters of the way down the long, straight road, I turned to look back at my sweet home. I thought of it as "my sweet home" because in that dwelling I was treasured, loved, nurtured, and probably, since I was an only child, a bit spoiled. I knew I pretty much had the run of the house and the land around it. It never occurred to me that I was an "only child." I had Blackie, silky soft and a great playmate.

I squinted in the fine light of the setting sun, seeing only dimly, and in a sort of dream, the small rock house that sat alone in a flat Texas pasture, surrounded by a windmill, a large water tank, and numerous chicken coops. I expect by that time of my life, I was in great need of glasses, but my proud father assured me that no child of his would ever need to rely on glasses. In the country school I attended, I sat close to the front of Mrs. Allen's classroom, peering at hieroglyphics on the chalkboard. My report card always came up with straight A's, except for behavior, which meant I talked to most anyone whenever I wanted. One could only imagine how much I might have learned if clear vision had been a priority to my father.

Blackie, a small spaniel built for water but living in a dry land, followed me both on and off the road, kicking up small stones and tearing through the low-to-the-earth weeds and flowers, carefully avoiding frequent prickly pear cacti. Blackie went everywhere I went. I admired his ability to smell his way through the world. We had already thoroughly explored the acreage near our rock house in the westerly direction of Twin Mountains; the easterly direction of small towns Talpa and Ballinger; and the northerly direction of Genevieve and Alf Smith's dairy farm.

On that particular day, we were headed in the southerly direction down the road to the cattle guard, which I was forbidden to cross because of its proximity to the highway. Across the highway was Goodfellow Air Force Base from which airplanes took off with a noisy regularity. I was one of the first people, along with Blackie, to reach the scene of a small airplane crash. The plane had taken off from the airstrip, crossed the highway in a customary manner, and done an immediate nose dive into our east pasture. The pilot got out, dusted his hands off, and walked away—to report the problem, I surmised. I knew from what I could see that the radio inside the plane wouldn't be much good for that. Blackie and I circled the plane, amazed at the absence of its nose that was either crushed or buried underground. As soon as people arrived, making the scene distracting and confusing, we headed home to get long drinks of water. Airline destruction evaluation made us very thirsty.

At the cattle guard we either turned around back toward home or we waited for my daddy. I suspected he had probably stopped off at the St. Angelus coffee shop to visit with his friends, Riley and Cooter. Sometimes he took me along for the ride; I read the newspaper headlines and funny papers while they talked about selling tires or running a dry cleaning business. My daddy was the tire salesman; his territory went all the way to Midland and back, through oil wells that smelled up the earth and blackened the skies. I was glad where I lived the sky was blue and the earth smelled good to Blackie.

Twin Mountains were far enough away to remain in my curiosity but near enough to be familiar and friendly. The sun made an attempt to set between them each night, never quite making its exact target, but Blackie and I cheered it on. We had some idea that the earth would turn just right one day, and we knew we'd be there to see it happen. At least, we thought we would. But lately, we weren't so sure.

There had been some changes in our lives recently. My friend, sixteen-year-old neighbor Loma Mae, invited me to stay overnight in her bedroom when they took my mother to the hospital. One night turned into a week because my mother didn't come home as soon as I would have liked. Loma Mae and I made bread, gathered eggs from reluctant chickens, pressed wildflowers in a book for her school project, and looked at movie magazines. It seemed like an extended holiday.

I didn't want to be a rude house guest, but I wanted to see my mother.

I guess I must have asked about a dozen times before they finally relented and said okay. We tied up Blackie with a short cord that was only as long as his face, which made my stomach feel sad, and drove to town. The hospital smelled like ether. I knew about ether. I'd had my tonsils out when I was five and remembered fighting to avoid the ether mask in the operating room. I was glad to see my mother didn't have to fight to breathe.

She lay very quiet in a tall bed. The Venetian blinds were almost closed. Light filtered in small slits in which dust particles danced. I watched them for a while and realized that they were the only movement in the room. My mother was covered with a clean sheet and light blanket up to her chest. I thought she looked comfortable and peaceful. I called her name and held her hand, but she didn't seem to want to talk to me right then. I told her about making bread and gathering eggs. I assured her that I wasn't afraid of Mrs. Smith's mean old rooster because I could run faster any day than his ugly claw feet could take him.

I put my fistful of red-orange Indian paintbrushes and blue-purple Texas bluebonnets into a glass by her bed. I told her when she woke up they would be the first things she'd lay eyes on, and she would know they came from me. I said I was sorry Blackie couldn't come to see her and explained that dogs weren't allowed to come into hospitals to lick the patients. I told her not to wake up now, she needed some rest. She was very still when I hugged her. I didn't say goodbye when I left because, at the time, I didn't know I needed to say goodbye.

My mother died seven days after having a massive cerebral hemorrhage, commonly known as a stroke, at the age of forty-three. She was survived by a loving husband, an eight-year-old daughter, and one small black dog.

MELISSA PALMER

Melissa had just turned 18 when her mother,
Peggy, died accidentally in 1995.

Things I forgot to tell you, too

I wonder sometimes if I could have stopped you long ago a life
ago the day you took the pills If I could have called to stop
the hand or hug you then stop you befriend you then I could
call you mom today so much unsaid when the last thing there was
was a beep on the machine and the heart was gone Did I ignore the
things you told me then
never gave up on you dream of it in guilt on nights so
long dreams of bee stings where you can't protect me they
swarm and dreams where I can't touch you wake to think
you're in the room beside me and I just can't breathe

I wonder sometimes if I wasn't eighteen I could have brought you
back from there guilty secret knew somehow you'd move on
when I was there and I tried and tried to keep you
too scared to say it loud then that back far in my mind I saw the
night dad would call and you'd be gone

I wonder sometimes if it's worth the work to hide the tears that come
in hours at night when I dream of a wedding day in years and I
will ready myself without you though you always taught me
to do my eyes
change the sad songs on the tuner
while it shouldn't be sad
think that you're journeying through something as I make a right turn
with that same radio song now a distant cry in my background
shrugging off the ice cream ad and Hallmark cards and once a year
calls from your friends and sisters

and sappy shows
the charade of forgetting the life I know
without you

Mom's Song

Singing the blues
with the car radio
I thought of you
years away remember
I would scream
MOMMY DON'T SING
So embarrassed
when you raised your
voice in song
What if someone hears you
I would think
Now alone in my car
I hear a song and
cry
Wondering if and when
I can ever hear
you again
Not in this life
at least
And it stings
My throat grows
dry and I picture
you entertaining
me
Stubborn daughter
tried so hard

to make me
smile

And now I
do WIDE EYED
without thought
of passing cars

For the record
You really were
a good singer

DIANE PAYNE

Diane was 18 when her mother, Betty Payne,
died in 1977 from breast cancer.

Shedding Hair

"Is the water too hot?" I ask Mom as she leans her head under the kitchen sink faucet.

"No, it's perfect."

Wearing only a stained polyester bathrobe and worn out slippers, Mom smiles as if she is a queen being treated to a head massage and shampoo. Not only do I want her to feel special, but I also want to be the one responsible for making her feel this way.

"Doesn't it feel good when the water trickles down your neck slowly?"

"Yeah. You're as good as the girls at Ottie's Beauty Shop. When you grow up, you'll be a good beautician."

"You mean that, Ma?"

"Yeah, you're already better than some of those girls."

"Really?"

"Yeah. Wait until you get older. You'll see. Some of the girls burn your scalp. Don't even check the water before sticking your head under. You won't be lazy like them. You got to let your nails grow though. That's what the women like. A nail massage."

"How long do they got to be?"

"Don't worry about that now. Looks cheap for girls your age to have long nails. I have never been able to grow nails. Don't know how those women do it. Don't know who cleans their ovens. They certainly ain't the ones doing it, not with those kind of nails."

While Mom talks, the sink fills with hair. I say nothing, hoping the hair will quit falling out. I don't know what to do. I'm afraid that it will all fall out if I keep scrubbing and I'm certain that the force of water coming out of the faucet will make her hair peel away like dead leaves shaking off a tree on a windy day. Mom keeps talking about her hairdressers as if she has enough hair to return there next Friday.

I towel dry what's left of Mom's hair as if nothing unusual has happened, hoping she won't turn her head and look at the sink filled with blackish gray hair. First she loses her breast and now her hair. And she's only thirty-three years old. That seems old to me but not old enough to be dying and losing parts of your body. As I pat Mom's hair dry, I try to say how clean her scalp smells but the tears begin to build and the words are choking up inside me.

"What's wrong?"

"Nothing, Ma. Nothing."

"Thought you were crying there for a minute," she says while I hold the towel tightly over her head, praying that when I remove it God will have grown her a new batch of hair, hair that will stay attached to her scalp. When I remove the towel, I expect a miracle. Instead there is even more hair clinging to the towel. I blame myself for every hair that falls out. If I hadn't washed her hair, it would still be there. Then I remember the hair on her pillowcase and blame God. God is supposed to be a miracle worker but I don't know who he saves those miracles for.

Before Mom sat down to have her hair washed, she had hair. Within minutes her hair fell out in clumps and left her with bald spots. I pick up a curler and try to wrap the remaining hair. Slowly the hair wraps around the sponge and I snap the curler in place, praying that the hair will quit falling out.

"You don't have to wrap it too tight," Mom says.

"I won't, Ma. Does this feel all right?"

"Perfect."

It's working better than I expected. Six curlers are in her hair and she doesn't look too bald with the hair wet and bunched up in curlers. I put a few more in and wonder how I'll be able to keep her away from the mirror. I wanted to make her feel good, feel queenly, but it's not going to work out that way.

"Can you tell that I'm losing any hair?"

This question takes me by surprise. She has never talked about it before. "Yeah, but it's not too bad."

"Not yet," she says. "Just about everyone going to therapy is bald. But it grows back. They say it'll grow back thicker than before."

"How long does it take for the hair to fall out?"

"Some say it fell out the very next day after the first treatment. Others don't even lose all of it, just some. Maybe I'll be one of the lucky ones."

"I hope so, Ma."

As I wrap the next curler, I remember my long hair and how good it felt when Mom brushed it. Last year the barber cut my hair off. Mom's arms had swollen from her cancer and my hair was becoming a nuisance. Mom moaned when she wrapped my hair into a tight bun and I moaned because my skin was stretched too tight for my eyes to fall back into their normal place. But at least she touched me when I had hair. When I went to the barber, I was hoping she would try to stop me, but she didn't. She took the bag of hair and put it in her bottom dresser drawer with all the other special things she saved.

"You ever miss your long hair?"

Her question frightens me. I'm sure she's reading my mind. "Not really, Ma." I lie but maybe she won't catch this one.

"Hair isn't that important, is it? We're lucky we have eyes. I'd hate to be blind or have polio. We got a lot to be thankful for, don't we?"

"Yeah, Ma."

After I wrap the last curler, Mom runs her fingers through her hair, checking the tightness of the curlers. "Let me see the mirror."

It is a hand mirror, the kind with two sides—one a regular mirror and the other a magnifier. First she looks through the magnifier side, then the regular, then back to the magnifier. Then she looks at me. I remain quiet. She looks at the floor and sees all the hair that has fallen and cries, forgetting the blindness and polio, only seeing baldness.

"Ma, I'm going to let my hair grow back long, longer than before. I'm going to make a wig for you."

She cries but says nothing.

"Ma, you're still beautiful. You got to believe that. I still love you, no matter what. There's still some hair left. It will curl. It's not all gone. Yours will grow back thick, remember? Soon it'll be the length of mine. Ma, it ain't forever. Stop crying, please. It's just hair."

We both know there will be none left when the hair dries and the curlers are pulled out. Each curler wrapped in five strands of hair will unravel and fall to the ground, joining the rest. Unlike my short hair, her head will be bald. Mom is thinking about beauty, yet I know that having hair means being touched. What Mom is going to miss are the trips to the beauty shop, her sisters dyeing it, and even my washing and setting it. Suddenly, my short hair feels long and I know I'll let it grow to make that wig.

Cindy was 22 months old when her mother,
Joy DeFehr, died by suicide in 1959.

Inheritance

My mother's picture sat atop the family piano.
My gaze would drift upward, as I lost myself
in her eyes. I would will her to look down at me.
I longed for one small piece of true memory.
Only her jewelry box had been saved, empty.
I would open the blue velvet compartments
look into the mirror that once held her reflection.
She was beautiful. So beautiful she became
a story to me, someone else's version of a person.
But beauty didn't save her, leaving me with the words
Suicide, Insanity. They have hands that reach out
to slap my face. Why was I not enough for her to stay?
Questions fall like so many pellets of icy rain.
In my own stubborn answer, I stay. To see my babies
born and grow, and watch her parents slip away.
To find the wrinkles in my own hands,
to love a man into middle age.

RACHEL E. PRAY

Rachel was 17 when her mother, Ellen Egger,
died in 1983 from breast cancer.

1983

for Ellen

Sharp scent of frozen rain, fresh-turned red
earth thrown on her open grave, plain wooden
coffin etched with a simple star.
Born in Iowa, Episcopal Church, buried a Jew
on a whaling island, my mother chose
her epitaph from Chaucer: "And gladly wolde she learne
and gladly teache," in the barren winter ground
beneath a stone.

Young men with Uzis edge the Negev
fields—here it is spring. I harvest oranges
bigger than my fist, gather avocados deep in shaded groves
prune countless peach buds, fingers stained
dusk-rose and faintly sweet. Delicate white blossoms
limned by light, the bony breast of earth
lifts to the sun, another morning
motherless.

REDA RACKLEY

Reda was 16 when her mother, Mary Reba
Harrison, died from colon cancer in January 1973.

The Grapefruit

Mama was old when she died so young. She was always saying, "I'm bone tired, I'm just plain-out bone tired." Every week the same ritual took place, Mama would pull out her old worn-out girdle, slip into the green polyester dress she made herself, put on the only makeup she ever wore, Avon's Orange Sunrise lipstick. Then, she'd climb into the '67 Dodge Dart and off she'd go to town to see old Dr. Hancock. Dr. Hancock never did figure out what was wrong with Mama. He'd just send her home with a new prescription from Cairo Pharmacy and she'd line that little brown bottle up with all the others. I'd watch her yank and pull herself out of the girdle, take her green dress off, and lay her burdensome body on the bed.

Well, finally Dr. Hancock wised up and sent Mama to a specialist over in Tallahassee. The doctor there said to my mama, "Reba we are going to have to do some exploratory surgery." Well, they did just that and in their great exploration they found a tumor. The doctor walked into the waiting room where me and my seven brothers and sisters and my daddy were waiting, and he said, "Mr. Rackley, we found a tumor the size of a grapefruit." That doctor said it kinda like it was a prize or something. What he didn't tell us at the time was it was cancerous and she'd be dead in three months.

I was fifteen years old then and it's come to me now that at age forty-three, that that tumor was a prize. Kind of like, you know, those piñatas kids have at their parties and all these treasures live inside and when you crack them open the goodies come tumbling to the ground and everyone scrambles to get a piece of candy, a trinket, a treasure. I think that inside that tumor was my mama's dreams, her desires, her hopes, her sadness, her weariness, her passion. Everything she could not say lived inside that tumor. That tumor became the vessel, the precious cauldron of her un-lived life.

About a year ago around my mama's birthday, I was at the grocery store in the produce department and my eye caught this huge pyramid of grapefruits. I walked over to the stack and I picked the one on the very top and put it in my cart, and then I picked up another one, and then another one, and pretty soon I must've had fifty of those yellow fruits in my cart. I turned around and I wheeled my cart to the checkout counter and started putting those little yellow balls on the conveyor belt. The checkout person looked at me like I was crazy and he said, "You know we do sell these by the bag." I just looked at him and said, "Yea, I know."

Well, they bagged my fifty grapefruits. I brought them home. I put them in the fruit bowl, the salad bowl, the mixing bowls, any bowl I could find. And there they were lined up on my kitchen counter. The crazy thing is I don't even like grapefruit. But, then, I couldn't get enough of them.

The next morning I go downstairs and I cut into the pink fleshy fruit. I am about to place this morsel in my mouth, when, all of a sudden, my hands flew to my heart and a knowing landed deep inside my belly. I gasped. I realized by eating all those grapefruit, I was trying to taste my mama, to sense her, to feel her inside me again. I wanted to know her dreams, her passions, her stories, the stories that were never told, 'cause she took them to her grave.

As I took the last bit of grapefruit, the juice ran down my face mixing with the salty tears now rolling from my eyes. I got up from the kitchen table and walked over to the mirror hanging over the fireplace. I looked inside that mirror and I saw my mama looking at me through my eyes. I gently placed my two fingers to my lips and then I reached out and touched the face of the woman looking at me. I smiled, she smiled, and then I heard her say, "Reda, don't ever give up on yourself, don't ever give up your dreams, don't ever stop believing in yourself. I know who you are, daughter. I gave birth to you and I know who you are." I turned away from the mirror and knew I was the voice of my mother. I was the keeper of her stories. I turned away from that mirror and turned towards embracing life in all of her glory, in all of her pain, in all of everything that crosses my path this lifetime. I am my mother's daughter and I will live to tell the stories.

Deidra was two and a half when
her mother, Lorraine, died from
complications of diabetes in 1974.

What Remains

Your life was a black eyelet dress
swaying in the June breeze.
My wavering baby heel touched down
on the low hem and slowly unraveled it.

Mama, they say this would have happened even if I was not born.
Too many years of illness had worn the fabric thin.
Still, I live my life doubly. Every memory I have is borrowed.
I stumble over what you left behind.

There are Japanese charms, shorthand manuals,
and a recipe for rhubarb strudel. There are tiny jars
of sequins and wrought iron candle holders.
There are things that stay inside me. They catch in my throat:
a piercing dread of illness, my tightrope walk of indecision,
the raw question—will my life end too soon?

Sweet warrior, Mama, when you knew that your life
was a battle you would lose, you became a tiger lily
dancing in a dark garden. You sang to me and told stories,
carried me back and forth across the shadows of the room,
and fed me dreams like bread from the oven.

Now, when the breeze whispers in June, I remember things I never knew.
Sometimes I stretch my hands toward yours and the air collapses.
But there are days, Mama, when the wind holds me together
with bright flowers and baby shoes and bits of black thread.
I stand where I am, in the center of what remains, and I begin to dance.

Laura was four in 1960 when her mother,
Sheila Craig Steen, died by suicide, a result of
improperly treated postpartum depression.

Bearings

I place the pieces of bone
cut by the dentist
from my number 17 molar
to prepare my crown
into the garden with my hollyhocks.
Maybe I should put the
baby teeth of my children
there too, empty the envelopes
addressed to Grace,
my tooth fairy alias.
My mother's teeth were
extracted, then she
had my sister, then she
extracted herself from
this world.

Bits of my bone
fall on my hollyhocks,
bone that grew
from milk, cheese, and Grape-Nuts
apples, tea, bread.
Did my mother leave
pennies under my pillow,
dimes, nickels?
Did I believe in the
tooth fairy
so much that I became one,

flying my children's teeth
to the castle of old teeth,
just the perfect size for Tom Thumb,
just enough enamel
to make them shine?

DIANA ROSEN

*Diana was 17 when her mother, Mae Zeidman
Rosen, died in 1961 of a cerebral hemorrhage.*

Sitting Shiva

I take extra care today to make sure
sheets are tucked underneath the mattress,
the bedspread draped evenly all around,
pillows fluffed, upright, at the headboard,
the room ready for company.

I supervise the kitchen like she did
directing people to dishes
in that cupboard,
silverware in this drawer,
napkins on the table over here.

Food, plates, candlesticks
at the ready on the buffet.
Long-ago uncles mumble hellos,
forever-aunts wander about, numb.
Her still-shocked friends attempt comfort.

I walk through the mournful throng
sit by my just-made friends
whose duty brought them here
wondering what to say.
(It's okay, you don't have to stay.)

That first night, and every night of shiva,
the sunset is hot pink and gold

as our diminished family
pretends to eat dinner
at the usual time.

Shiva: Hebrew for seven, the number of days for mourning in Judaism.

Hands

Small, graceful, carefully manicured every Monday evening
while she sits in her Queen Anne chair next to the good floor lamp;
my mother's hands,
always holding the winning Gin Rummy cards,

or curved against staccato knitting needles
fashioning the woolen sweater she would never finish.
(It hangs still in my closet, a nubby gold remnant,
one arm missing, bodice half done.)

Aided by an antique silver and gold thimble, her fingers deftly
work the needle, creating embroidery stitches of vivid names,
her clear-polished forefinger pointing to the overturned sampler,
showing how perfection is not just on the surface.

Hands, purposeful and strong, guide the huge mangle
over brilliant white muslin sheets cascading into the willow basket
below. End-of-day hands hold Zane Grey novels read in deep of night,
her gentle husband oblivious in his easy slumber.

Hands smooth the maternity dress over a baby soon stillborn;
adjust the gas flame under the plum tomato sauce simmering
hours for a nearly exquisite flavor. Hands, held behind her, pull
her mouth into a line of unexplained fear or was it severe shyness?

At the gleaming mahogany secretary, she sits in constant anticipation, scribbling notes in her mammoth black leather notebook of recipes; writes to one sister in long-term care, to another of her heart's pain engraved as teeth marks on her navy Shaeffer fountain pen.

She lies on the smoothly vacuumed carpet beside the freshly made bed, unnoticed too long in that awful quiet of seeping blood vessels, hands in push-up position, trying to right herself. Hands cold. Rigid. Ready for the last task.

SAVINA AMICO ROXAS

Savina was 10 when her mother
died from tuberculosis.

Mother's Motto: It Was Just Meant to Be

Oh, Mother, do not say
it was meant to be.

Once more it is Easter
and you are not here.

My heart still shrinks
when I see the empty rocker

face the kitchen silence
hear only a faint echo

of your laughter as we chopped
hazelnuts and golden raisins

to knead into the risen dough
for the humped-back *panetone*.

The dogwood tree, heavy with blossoms
still wears the yellow and blue ribbons

tied around its trunk in remembrance
of that spring's shattered promise.

The steps where you fell, split
your bones, scarred my life, have memories

hard as the dried blood halo around
your head when I found you.

Oh, Mother, do not say
it was just meant to be.

Marjorie was seven when her mother,
Mabel Bowman Lagemann, died from leukemia
after 10 months of illness in 1936.

Two Days That Changed My Life

The Day My Mother Died

I woke up under the dining room table. I had never slept there before, but it was so hot last night that Daddy said we could sleep downstairs on sheets. So when I woke up, I was surprised before I remembered. Bobby, my brother, was on the other side of the table. He was still asleep. Daddy was already up. I could hear him talking to the nurse in the kitchen. He said, "It's going to be another hot one." And she answered, "I'm afraid so." It was August before school started and real hot.

I went to see what they were fixing for breakfast. The nurse was chopping up ice to put in the bag for my mother. Daddy was squeezing orange juice. I asked for a piece of ice in my juice. The nurse gave me a piece and Daddy put the glass on the nook table. He told me to go upstairs and wash up first. At the bottom of the stairs I looked in the mirror on the closet door. Boy, was I a mess! Before I went to bed last night I had a purple Popsicle and I had purple rivers on my arms and purple all around my mouth. I ran upstairs and really washed my face and arms and even my knees.

When I went into my room to get a clean sunsuit, I saw Mommy was still asleep. She was in my bed. I tried to make her wake up, but she wouldn't. Yesterday she wouldn't wake up either because she was in a coma. That's when you sleep so hard nobody can wake you up. I hoped that when she did wake up she would be all well.

She'd been sick since last fall when I was in first grade. Daddy took her to the best hospital in St. Louis where she stayed until she came home in May. Then she got sick again and had to go to the Methodist Hospital. At first, last fall when she was in the hospital, I felt lonely and tried to eat the food the housekeeper fixed. I didn't feel like eating without Mommy, not even the breakfast that Daddy fixed.

Well, I had to get dressed. The fan on the dresser blew my hair every which way and made a sound like buzzing bees. I was almost afraid to get close to it to open the drawer. Bobby told me if you stick your finger in the fan it would cut it right off. So I was careful. I don't like the fan but the nurse said it keeps Mommy cool.

After I put on the clean sunsuit, I tried to comb my hair. I went over to Mommy again and shook her arm to see if she would wake up and comb my hair. But she didn't, and I knew I would have to do it myself. It didn't look good. When the nurse came up, I asked her if she would do it after she put the ice bag on Mommy's forehead and cooled her off with a wet washrag. She did.

I went downstairs and had orange juice with more ice in it and Rice Krispies. I wished Mommy would wake up so we could giggle like we did the day before she had the coma. She talked funny that day because her tongue was swollen. She laughed about it and we did too. She had to drink out of a bent straw. I read to her about Skaggs the milk horse, and Bobby read to her from his book. Later, we played Rummy and we laughed and laughed. The nurse said we were wearing her out. Mommy said we weren't. Then Daddy said it was his turn to talk to her. I kissed her on the nose and said "Toodle-Ooh!" We did that sometimes to be silly. She smiled and said "Toodle-Ooh" to me.

After I ate my breakfast, I went outside to swing. Pretty soon I heard some kids next door, and we decided to play "Tappy on the Icebox." I ran to hide behind the Alandt's garage and stepped on something sharp like a nail. Ouch, did that hurt! My foot was bleeding. I ran home as fast as I could and went upstairs to the bathroom. I sat on the edge of the washbowl so I could wash the dirt off. I went barefoot all week so my foot was pretty dirty. I scrubbed and scrubbed with Lifebuoy soap until it was clean and I washed the rest of my leg too. I knew that Mommy would have done it so I got the iodine and put the stick thing in the hole. Ow! That hurt even more.

Before I could put a bandage on it, the nurse came in to see what I was doing. (I think I cried a little from the iodine.) She washed it some more and put more iodine on it. Then she put the bandage on with adhesive tape. I tried not to cry but it hurt. She decided I needed to wash the other foot and leg and put on clean socks and shoes. She was nice and tried to make Mommy feel better.

I went into my bedroom again to see if Mommy was awake yet. She was snoring real loud. I had never heard her do that before. Daddy was standing by the window looking out at the street. I saw tears go down his face. I felt scared and sad. Daddies don't cry. I took hold of his fingers and stood there by him. Pretty soon we saw Iris Meyer's car come up and stop in front of the house. Iris was a friend of Mommy's and they were sorority sisters. I ran downstairs to tell her Mommy was in a coma and Daddy was upstairs.

She came upstairs and held Mommy's hand and said, "I'm so sorry, Al." He said, "Thank you for taking Bob and Margie." I was surprised because nobody told me I was going anywhere. The nurse came in and told Daddy she had our suitcases packed. I didn't want to go and started to say so but Bob came in and yelled he wasn't going. Iris and Daddy told him he had to go whether he wanted to or not. I just kept quiet. I kissed Mommy goodbye on the forehead. She smelled like hair oil and her face was sweaty. She was still snoring even louder. We went downstairs and got in Iris' car. We sat in the back seat and didn't say anything. Bob looked real mad and turned his face away. I was scared.

Iris fixed us lunch with Martha Lois, who was five, and Paul, the Daddy. Bob went upstairs to read. Martha Lois and I played dolls. Iris said she would turn the hose on us after a while so we could cool off. Martha Lois and I went across the street to tell Virginia, she was six, and her sister, Nancy, she was four, that they could go under the hose with us. I was the oldest. I was seven. Martha Lois told them my mommy was real sick and I was going to stay at her house. I said it was just 'till Mommy got well.

We had so much fun sprinkling each other I forgot all about Mommy being sick. Iris put a little table out and we had cookies and Kool-Aid and told stories. Bob didn't want to play under the hose or eat cookies. He just sat on the front porch on one of the cement benches and read his book until supper.

I told Iris about my foot and showed her the wet bandage. She took it off and washed my foot again and put Mercurochrome on it. I told her iodine is better. She put another bandage on and said I had to wear socks and shoes. Martha Lois could still go barefoot. We ate supper in the kitchen and Paul tried to cheer up everybody by making a spider with his fingers. Bob wouldn't talk or laugh.

Then after supper, Iris called Bob and me to come sit on the benches on the porch. She said she had something important to tell us. I tried to guess. I thought it might be something fun. She put her arm around me and said, "Your mother's in heaven." Bob asked, "When did she die?" Iris said it was right after we left. Bob yelled at her, "Why didn't you tell us? I knew it would happen!" and ran in the house. I just sat there. I couldn't think of anything to say. Iris hugged me and we just sat on the bench and listened to the bugs.

That night, because it was still so hot, Iris and Paul said we could sleep downstairs in the living room. I lay there a long time listening to the bugs outside and to everyone breathing. I kept thinking that I didn't have a mother anymore; that she had died. I wondered what you did if you didn't have a mother. I remembered what Iris said and wondered where heaven really was. What was it like? What was Mommy doing? I wanted to be with her. I cried a little, but not out loud so anyone would hear me. Finally, I went to sleep.

The Funeral

We had to sit very still. Daddy said so. Bobby sat on one side of Daddy and I sat between Daddy and Aunt Maude. She's Mommy's sister. I was afraid I would get sick and throw up. I felt like it because it was real hot, and it smelled like too many flowers. There were lots of them all around the coffin. That's where Mommy was—in the coffin. There were big fans on poles like lamps and they turned and made humming noises. There were lots of people. They talked very quietly. Some of them whispered. So I knew I had to be quiet and sit still.

For a while I did sit still. I tried to sit up straight like I was in school. Then, the minister began to talk about Mabel—that was my mother's name. Alfred was Daddy's. The minister kept on talking. Pretty soon I got tired of listening. I just couldn't sit still. So I began to swing my feet and think about my pretty new shoes. They were patent leather and shiny. Daddy bought them for me at Ayres the week before Mommy died. I stuck my legs straight out and looked at my new white socks with flowers on the cuffs. I swung my feet some more. They felt cooler that way. Then Aunt Maude put her hand on my knee and I couldn't swing my feet anymore.

I was sure I would throw up if I had to sit still and smell the flowers and listen to the minister. 'Specially if I couldn't even swing my feet.

Then the minister said we could come up to the coffin for a last viewing. I wasn't sure what he meant. Viewing just means to look at something. Bobby looked at me and reached for my hand. I didn't really want to look again, but he kinda pulled me and it was better than just sitting. So we stood right by the coffin and looked. I didn't like to see Mommy dressed up and lying in a coffin. I wanted her to sit up and smile or laugh and say it was a joke. But she didn't move at all. She had lots of powder and rouge on her face. Her hair was in neat waves. It didn't look right. She had on a pink dress. The shiny pillow and puffy bed looked soft and comfortable. Part of the coffin lid was down and I looked under it to see if she had on shoes in bed. She didn't. She had on pink slippers. Then, I felt real sad because I knew it was the last time I would see her. After we went back and sat down two men closed the lid and I knew nobody would ever see her again. Tears came down my face but I didn't cry out loud at the funeral.

Then someone played some organ music and we got up. I watched them carry the coffin out to put it in a real big car. It was called a limousine. We got in the car and the coffin was in the back. I wanted to yell real loud to Mommy to push the lid open and get out. Daddy and Bobby didn't say anything. I could tell by the look on Daddy's face that I had better sit still and not say a word. So Bobby and Daddy and I sat still and looked straight ahead at the policemen on motorcycles. Nobody talked, not even the driver. Bobby and I didn't even talk about the policemen. I wanted to. They had flags on their handlebars.

When we got to the cemetery all of a sudden there were lots of people. They drove their own cars, I guess. I saw lots of Mommy's friends and relatives. Grandma and Grandpa and Aunt Maude and the Poppaws and Elva Hageman. They came from Ohio. Not Grandma and Grandpa—they came from Danville, Illinois, on the train. I saw them at the funeral. The Andersons and the Myers were there and even the Alandts from next door. None of their kids came, though. Only Bob and me. We were the only kids.

They took the coffin and put it by a hole in the ground. It was a neat hole with straight sides. I wondered how they dug it so straight. There were strings along the sides and a man cut the strings. Then they put the coffin on a contraption that lowered it slowly into the hole. They had a crank to turn that made it go down. The minister, that was the man that talked about Mabel, said something terrible—that we are ashes to ashes, dust to dust. Mommy wasn't ashes and dust. She was a real person. I didn't like that. Then Daddy took dirt and dropped it on the coffin lid. It made a loud plopping noise. Everyone turned around and walked away from the grave. They all began to talk. They left Mommy there and started to walk to their cars like it was all over. I guess it was. The men shoveled more dirt over it. I didn't want to look at that and I didn't want to hear the dirt falling on the coffin. So I went and stood by Daddy. He was talking to some of his teacher friends.

One of them asked Daddy what he was going to do with the children. So I held his hand and listened. I just thought we would go home and I would go back to School #58 next week with Bobby. But he said he was going to take Bobby to live in Missouri where his brother has a farm. That's Uncle Walter. I wanted him to say I would go too. I wanted to go where Bobby went. But he said I was going to live with Iris and Paul Myers. I didn't want to. We weren't going to live in our own house anymore. That was awful. I thought, "I don't have a family anymore. My mother is dead and Bobby is going to go live on the farm with all our Lagemann cousins and I have to go live with people who aren't even related." I begged Daddy to let me go to Uncle Walter's too. He said, "No," and sounded cross. So I knew it was settled.

We left the cemetery and got back to our house where Aunt Maude and Grandma and some of the women fixed lunch for everyone. I helped them. They had ham and potato salad, two of Mommy's favorite things. I wished she was there in the kitchen, too, where all the women were. It was her kitchen, anyway. They didn't even know where anything was so I had to tell them. I put out knives and forks and plates for people just to pick up on the nook table in the kitchen. They ate in the living room and the dining room and even in the kitchen. Mommy wouldn't have liked it that they ate in the living room. They all talked about Mabel. Someone said, "The good always die young." That was scary. I tried to be good and maybe that would happen to me.

Then Grandma and Grandpa, and Aunt Maude and the rest all said goodbye to me and I had to take my things in a suitcase and get in the car with Paul and Iris Myers. Daddy put my bike in the back seat. Martha Lois, their daughter, who was only five, didn't get to come to the funeral. I guess she was too little. So I sat in the front with Iris and Paul. I didn't want to say goodbye to Daddy and Bobby and go away to live in the Myers' house. It was scary and I felt like throwing up. But I knew I had better not. They kept talking to me so I wouldn't cry. I had to be brave.

They said next week I would have to go to School #1. Iris said Daddy will live in an apartment on Thirty-eighth Street. I didn't know where that was. Everything was wrong. I couldn't believe what was happening. I couldn't believe we wouldn't even live together in our house on Maple Lane. I wondered if I would ever get to live there again. I knew nothing would ever be the same. I sat very still and listened. I didn't throw up and I didn't cry.

CAROLE STONE

Carole was five when her mother,
Margaret, died of rheumatic fever,
four months after her father's death.

Lost Tongue

Sometimes I feel I could speak
a lost tongue, the way as a girl

in downtown department stores I would trail
two chatting women through cosmetics,

eavesdropping on their Hungarian,
as if, like an incantation,

those dimly remembered sounds
would make my mother appear.

And sometimes syllables drip
from my weeping mouth like water,

making first helpless utterances
that called forth a mother's love.

It's Easy to Imagine You Here

Amid the Spanish tile, by the oversized pool where
Esther Williams once swam laps, you come back, Mother,
my movie star, sipping a frozen daiquiri,
your long pearls translucent in your pink silk lap.

Now I see you poised at the pool's edge
in your one-piece wool bathing suit.
Legs slick with coconut oil,
you dive and disappear as you did when I was four.

I hold my breath, afraid this will be the end
of my imagining, until you surface, wave to me.
Now you hold me in your underwater world.
Longer and longer I stay with you before you vanish

again, Mother, my mermaid, and lungs bursting
I must kick to the pool's top where
on the billboard the peeling figures
of movie actresses hold foaming daiquiris.

Jennifer was 13 when her mother, an alcoholic,
died of renal failure in 1947.

Electra's Curse

"Why am I the only one that wears blue?"

"It is the colour of the wind. It is the
colour of what goes away and is never coming
back, but which is always here, waiting like
death among us. It is the colour of the dead."

The Woman Who Rode Away
—D.H. Lawrence

Sometime in April 1947, I attended the funeral of my mother. My mother's name was Kirsten. My father called her Kiki. After World War II, my mother divorced my father but it was too late, she died anyway. We were both quite young at the time. She was nearly forty-four and I was nearly fourteen.

Most of that eighth grade year I attended Miss Evelyn Drearson Muffy's Ranch School for Girls, somewhere in the center of California. I thought I was going to spend Easter vacation with Anna and with her son, Nathaniel. Nathaniel didn't talk to me much anymore because he was post-puberty but his mother made up for that. Anna was my mother's best friend and she lived in a beach house and survived on a shoestring. She could make anything out of nothing. During my Christmas vacation earlier that school year, while I was staying at her house, she told me my mother was in a sanitarium. Anna hadn't written to me since Christmas, still I knew my mother had left the sanitarium and gone back to the desert to live with my father. Somebody always tells you that stuff.

When I got to Anna's house for Easter, I was having a fit to show her my new sandals and my Indian print dress. Nathaniel looked at me funny and didn't say anything at all. He usually said something, even now that we were old. Anna took me for a walk and told me my mother was dead and I sat down on a stone wall for a while. After that I went to bed in Anna's room and she told everyone to leave me alone.

Anna and I took a train back to Arizona for the funeral. I never stopped talking the whole time. Anna made me drink her brandy. All the way from the seashore back to the desert, all the while I was talking to Anna without stopping. I kept thinking my father would be noble and tragic and meet our train and say something profound. He was in the kitchen in his bathrobe. He was very drunk and maudlin and he began crying out to me as if I were an adult. Anna was furious with him.

I don't remember anything else until the next morning when we drove to the mortuary. I screamed and yelled and wouldn't get out of the car. My father had to drag me. I told everyone it was my nine-year-old brother who screamed and yelled like that. I told everyone that for years. That's still the way I tell it sometimes. After we got inside the funeral parlor I could see my mother on a blue dais. She was laid out for everyone to see, and everything was blue with blue lights, so even the flowers looked blue and it was like the last morning.

Then I don't remember anything until the gravesite and my father pulling out his great German pistol and threatening to shoot himself. I remember thinking how undignified he was, but mostly how it made me sick the way he upstaged my mother all her life and now he couldn't even let her have the center of attention when she was getting buried for crissake. My brother never said a word that I can remember. My sister said some things, but I didn't care. I went back to Anna's and then back to Evelyn Drearson Muffy's.

I really remember that school. I mean it was the sort of place you never forget. It was deep in the woods somewhere and all the teachers lived in little houses with Siamese cats. I was stuck in one cottage with the sixth and seventh grades, about fourteen of us all day. The teacher read us *Ramona* every afternoon. Evelyn Drearson Muffy lined us up before dinner and we blew in her face to prove we hadn't been smoking. Friday nights there was a dance in the living room. A few boys came to visit the older girls. The rest of us had to dance with each other. I had an awful old-fashioned formal with puffed sleeves. It was a kind of blue brocade my mother bought the summer before. It did have long sleeves to start with, but she took them apart and made the puffed ones. God, she even bought me bloomer gym shorts in the seventh grade in a public school because she thought they were quaint. I bought a straight pair without her knowing. Anyway, most of the girls wore strapless dresses to the Friday night dances and there I was, looking like the turn of the century.

Some girls in the high school used to sneak out and meet boys at night. They cut their window screens at the edges and then tucked them back so no one could tell they were loose. I was afraid if Miss Muffy ever found out she would call me in for questioning. She gave me the old third degree once, in regard to some missing cupcakes. She shamed it out of me. She had one of those looks you don't see much these days. All the girls did to me was short-sheet my bed and take my extra food but they said I better keep my mouth shut in the future. I wanted to quit riding after that because the girls always went bareback or went swimming nude or took the horses in the river with them. That stuff was strictly against the rules and I was a lousy liar. Old Miss Muffy had a weird eye. Finally I took a bad fall off my horse. We slipped in the mud actually. I said I was afraid of horses and so I got permission to quit. I went for walks instead. I wandered off into the hills and sat on the rocks like a reptile in the sun.

After my mother died that spring, things got easier. I went around very silent and tragic for a while. You get more respect when someone dies. The only thing, I got poison oak so bad I couldn't sleep. They tied my hands so I couldn't hurt myself. I didn't go for walks anymore. Miss Muffy called me in to tell me about death and about going on because, after all, my mother would have wanted me to. It was very embarrassing.

I didn't have to ride anymore and that was fine with me. I did miss one girl with dark red hair. She was an Amazon when she was riding. She was the same color as the horse. She always left the stable with an English saddle, boots, whip, and everything. Then she would throw everything down under a tree, toss a rope around her horse's neck, and jump barefoot onto his bare back. Then she would ride out into the water nearly nude, sometimes swimming beside her horse, his mane and her hair the same dark color on the water. After I quit riding, she did come to my room a few times to sit and comb out her thick matted hair. It took a long time. She used a grooming comb from the stable. Sometimes she found a tick.

I began to read a lot. I started talking to myself. There was a long rock in the middle of a stream surrounded by beds of stones and rushing water. No poison oak in the water. I went there every day and I sat. I read romantic poets and plays about problems. I decided I belonged in the theater. I began to see that arrogance and solitude were the best defense for me. I wrote poems and hid them. Edna St. Vincent Millay was my mother's contemporary almost. I reasoned that they both died of love. I read,

> Wine from these grapes I shall be treading,
> Morning and noon and night until I die,
> Stained with these grapes, I shall lie down to die.

What that had to do with my mother's bourbon and Camel cigarettes I'm not sure but it seemed to fit.

In June we had to graduate. The eighth grade wore white formals with long sleeves. We carried a daisy chain. The seniors wore pastel dresses and carried a chain of dark red roses. I recited a Longfellow poem about the road of life and broken steps where the feet seek to climb. I got a part in the play. I played an old man. Whenever there was a crisis, I rode onstage on a jackass and tolled a bell, fell down on the lawn, and rolled down a hill.

The day of the ceremonies Evelyn Drearson Muffy dressed in a rusty amber gown with amber beads and her hair was done in a Pre-Raphaelite style. As we began our slow procession to the amphitheater in the trees, we crossed the road leading from the school gate. It was a twisting lane, I remember, cut out of the trees so that the branches overhead were locked together. Just as Miss Muffy reached the edge of the lane at the head of our procession, my father's blue convertible roared around the curve full of drunken friends and two large boxer dogs. Miss Muffy stepped forward and raised an imperious arm. The honking ceased but my father put on an act all that afternoon, imitating Miss Muffy raising her arm like Caesar to halt the progress of the barbarians.

It's odd though. Eight years later, in college, again in a woman's school and finally in black, I looked up automatically from the small Greek theater and there he was again, of course, coming over the top of the hill high above the rows of stone steps. He only had one dog that time. It was the last time I let him get away with it. Very F. Scott Fitzgerald hoopla, Anna always said about him. Scene stealing I call it.

He was overseas when I graduated from high school. He was somewhere in Korea sewing up the wounded so I got off the hook in '51. Everything went off without a hitch that night. I gave a speech with a theatrical tableau going on behind me. Arty as all hell. My whole class got drunk in a beach house belonging to Bette Davis. I spent the money my father sent on a chic dress instead of a phony formal. High school was great when it ended.

Anyway, we cleared out of Evelyn Drearson Muffy's that night back in 1947 and started to drive back to Arizona. We had a blowout on the road the next afternoon. We rolled all over the desert. My sister couldn't hold the car on the road. Twenty years old and she couldn't hold the car on the road. After we rolled over a few times and the car landed on its side, some Mexican railroad workers ran over from the tracks and hauled us out the windows. There was a lot of gas pouring out of the car so we scrambled up to the road as fast as we could. The trouble was we had all taken our shoes off in the car and when we got out on the sand our feet began to burn. We took off everything we had and stood on it until a car stopped. All of us were cut and bruised but most of all our feet were burnt. Our car didn't even explode after all but all my clothes and graduation presents were full of sand, even the stuff inside the suitcases.

When our feet healed enough so we could walk, my father sent me and my sister to a dude ranch in the mountains behind Tucson. I stayed most of that summer. A cowboy made passes at my sister. He was a grilled cheese blond with pure gold skin. He never wore a shirt. Once we stopped to swim and his legs were white as a baby's so I loved him somewhat more than my Amazon friend at school who was gold all over like a goddess. The cowboy flirted with my sister but his real girlfriend worked on the ranch. She was very direct in the way of western farm women and dead on the level as they say. Once someone called her out of the kitchen after she put the food on the table. She just laughed and said name your poison but get it yourself.

The woman who owned the ranch was a patient of my father's. She had arthritis. She could still ride a horse. I had to room with her daughter, which was awful as I was easily intimidated by girls. This daughter had good breasts and didn't talk. She wasn't mean though, not like the girls at school. She told me to pull my bed away from the wall and to empty my boots because of scorpions and centipedes and so on. Millipedes came up and out of the pipes in the bathtub if you didn't keep the plug in.

My sister had a room of her own. She got a room of her own because she always had a room of her own. My mother saw to that. Always my mother spoiled my sister. Then she told everyone how tough I was. She told everyone my sister had to have things just so but I could adjust to anything. I could go to public school or private. My sister had problems with hypochondria, megalomania, skin diseases, and diarrhea. She was also damn mean most of her life.

Anyway, that August I got the curse for the first time. I was only almost fourteen. I went to my sister for Kotex and the rest of that stuff. She was in bed eating. She looked at me and said did I really *need* it. She hadn't had any periods until she was sixteen. There was no store inside of forty miles so I went to the cowboy's girlfriend in the kitchen. She acted as if she were really worried about me and said how it was normal and natural and all that women's magazine stuff, but she was so nice I acted as if it were all some kind of big thing and mattered to me one way or the other. Anyway, I got to stay in the kitchen with her for a few days instead of riding horses all over hell. The rides were all right except you had to go with the cowboy and you had to trot all the time. Now I like a horse to walk or to canter. Trotting gives me a headache. After trotting for miles the cowboy would let us canter just before we got back to the stable. Once when I was going too fast to stop I heard his rope whistling over my shoulder and I saw a black tarantula on my horse's rump. The cowboy knocked it off with his rope. He was beautiful like the horses but I couldn't talk to him. I was happier in the kitchen where I could talk.

At the end of summer my father sent me to Tucson to live with another patient of his. That was fine with me. I didn't care if I never saw another mountain. I took drama lessons and went to the movies. In the ninth grade I graduated again. It was a three-year junior high. I had a sharkskin blue dress. That was a good year. I had a room of my own and public school was more fun. The teachers had more to say. They even said things like, "the eternal verities aren't so eternal anymore," and "in knowledge is much sorrow," and "thought breaks the heart." I had a music teacher who told me solemnly that it is better to have loved and lost than never to have loved at all. I was in lots of plays at Mary McMagic's Children's Theatre. I played the Scarecrow in the *Wizard of Oz*. In order to prove my superior brain power, I had to recite the alphabet backwards. I can still do it. I fell in love with the Cowardly Lion who was a high school senior and very handsome, but he fell in love with the Tin Woodsman.

The next year I went back to the mountains. My father had built a fort with a stockade all around it. There was flagstone set in blue cement. There was a long flight of flagstone steps leading up to the top of one wall and down to the outside. Every time someone drove in we had to open a double gate in the stockade but anyone could walk over the wall. My father was married and he had another daughter and she played on the flagstones where we mixed more blue cement. The fort was never finished while we lived there. They built a handball court first but then everyone had a bedroom and a bathroom and a fireplace but the kitchen was in the laundry rooms.

I made friends with the wife of a Mexican construction worker. She told me all about how dull sex was after you got married. Her husband let me mix cement. A local artist in the eighteenth year of his blue period painted our bathroom ceilings and walls with oil paint. Mine had seagulls and sea form on blue waves. I took care of my new baby sister and tried to set my hair and learned to drink Irish Mist with my father.

Finally my father's manic phase ended in general disaster. Everything collapsed in violence and ruin. I ran away a few times but I always came back. My father shot a man and broke his arm. He set the arm but that didn't help much in court. He was blackballed from the Rotary Club and funny things like that, and he was fouled up with another woman and very violent with my stepmother and with all of us. After the court case the axe fell and he lost his license to practice medicine in that state. It was like an Ibsen play. We left the fort late at night, driving back to the seashore, escaping again. My father shipped out to an island in the Pacific somewhere before anyone knew what he had done or why.

The day before we left I walked five or more miles into the desert to the graves. I looked for my mother's but I couldn't find it. I was sorry because I had sworn to myself that if I ever got out of this town I would never come back to this dead place in the desert.

I sat down on a stone like a reptile in the sun. I said, "Goodnight, Mrs. Calabash, wherever you are, and if I don't see you again remember I called. I know we killed you or he did, but what the hell, you asked for it."

On the way home I walked on the dirt road instead of through the cacti. My high school principal drove by and saw me. He stopped the car and his wife had that motherly look and didn't ask me where I'd been and I hated her for it. Her daughter was a friend of mine at school. Taught me to shave my legs. I wanted to tell her her daughter was a tramp if there ever was one. I wanted to tell them both what I really knew about their precious only daughter. But what difference did it make anyway. I was leaving and I was never coming back. I told them I didn't want a goddamn ride.

LAURIE MICHELLE SUMMER

*Laurie was nearly two when her
mother, Alice, died of complications
after a miscarriage in 1971.*

Dry Bones

I want to walk into my mother's kitchen,
walk into aromas of compassion and comfort—
    chicken soup simmering, brown bread baking,
her lavender lotion and perspiration
blending with scents of sustenance.

I want her to invite me to sit, sip tea.
I want to watch her chop up onions, peel carrots.
I want to see the tears
hastening down her cheeks as she works,
salt droplets flavoring the hot broth.

I want to be flooded with memories
while sitting at her table.
I want to be reminded of the time
when I was eight, and had the flu.
How she spooned warm liquid between my lips,
asked me if I'd like to watch cartoons.

I can almost see her.
Her face,
the softest moon,
her hands
the gentlest breeze.

I will never see her.

This fact still startles me,
startles me into
twenty-eight-year-old tears,
that I now shed, for my mother,
dead since I was two.

I stand before the stove in my kitchen,
immerse chicken bones into rough waters,
chop the onions and the carrots coarsely.
I let the aged wine of my sorrow
rain into my broth.

It feeds the hunger in my belly,
eases the drought
within these dry bones.

Mother's Day

  Your fingers turn
the shadowy pages of my memory.
  Long and slender,
the fingers play upon my soul,
striking keys deep within.
  I cannot remember you.

  I study your portrait,
hanging in my grandmother's living
  room. The dead hang
with the living. Ivory skin,
an open, waiting mouth, shiny brown eyes.
  My Snow White.

The fairest of
them all. You bit into the apple when
  I was but a chick.
No prince could wake you with a kiss.
I, alone in the nest,
  waiting, unable to fly.

  Remember you
I can't—and yet—I do,
  I must remember you, my mother.
Slender white fingers once
tickled me with love.
  Watchful eyes shone with warmth for me.

  Somewhere in a secret chamber,
treasures you bestowed to me.
  At moments when
the breeze is gentle, when the sun
shines in my eyes, when I
  am tickled with the Earth's love . . .

. . . I think of you . . .
. . . and remember . . .
. . . what cannot be remembered . . .

ZAHAVA ZOFIA SWEET

Zahava was nine in 1941 when her mother,
Esther Eckstein, was murdered in the Holocaust.

You Vanished

To my mother

I have learned the color of your absence,
the cloth that didn't wrap your body.
In an empty grave, I see your fingers
climbing the walls. Family members
you left went to their own graves.
I look for you. I want to know how you died.
I want to hear from your lips
that left many imprints on my face.
I want your hair spread around me once more.
But no! There is the black in my window.
And you? Drowned inside the sea?
Fish could feed on you. Long seaweeds
wrap around your body, corals attach
themselves to your belly.
It was not the ocean that took you.

I don't know who took you. I don't know why.
You disappeared one snowy night.
You went down the stairs from grandma's home.
The frost gripped you. Black arms seized you.
You vanished, not leaving a strand of your hair,
your familiar scent of konvalja.

They took you. They took your gold rings
and stole the black crown of your hair.

I stare at an old photo wrapped carefully
in a soft cloth. How would you be today?
I see you in the black crown of your hair,
your voice like the satin of my white Purim dress
whispers my name: Zosienko.
I am the girl in the snow queen gown
with hair straight straw and serious eyes,
the child who would slip a hand into yours
and be led for miles.

I go to a place in the forest.
So quiet here among the trees.
Your hair wraps around me like a shawl.
You carry a basket of wild strawberries
small as tear drops. And you collect driblets of rain.
They shine on green leaves. You take a berry
between your fingers, from your hand to my mouth.
A taste of blood.

Black Moss

I see her hair,
a black wave,
the verdant sponge
of the forest.

In her arms
she held me,
her hair
above my heart.

She played dolls with me
on the wooden floor
of Grandma's home.

A grandfather clock
swung its pendulum
to the moon and sun
to the moon and sun.

1941. The pendulum stood still.

She walks down the stairs
of Grandma's home
her black fur coat
in her arms.

She opens the door
and walks out
into the pinching cold
closing the door behind her.

I open the door
she had just closed,
step out next to her
and hold her hand.

Branches of an oak
gripped by frost.
Two men snatch her away,
walk her to the curb,
squeeze her into a car
with gray windows.

I want to say a word,
to yell,
but my voice
freezes in my throat.
My eyes are on her
footprints in the snow.

I turn back to the house,
walk to the front steps,
open the door
and return to
Grandmother's house.

Grandma's home is silent.
The table bare, the laughter gone,
the silver knives too
that blinked to the spoons.

Silent
as if black spiders
marked with blood
had crawled out of the walls.

No stone or pebble
mark her place in the earth
where I could bring
my flowers.

You must be somewhere,
someplace like the forest
where moss greets the eye.

I sit under a tree,
my body curved to its trunk,
and I lay out the flowers.

Each one heavy in my hand.
Each one placed lightly onto
the receptive earth.

Marian was 14 days short of her fourth birthday
when her mother, Katherine Tieszen Kleinsasser,
died from a postpartum hemorrhage in 1937.

Planting the Garden

On the great Central Plain
in the state of South Dakota,
southeast corner,
my grandfather Kleinsasser staked his claim
to 160 acres of six-feet-high prairie
near a town to be named Freeman in 1879.

Yankton Sioux still roamed that land,
and one surprised my grandmother in her sod-house
kitchen at noon time.
Not knowing his language, she offered him
a slice of warm bread with mulberry-rhubarb jam,
which he accepted and went his way.

It was a land inhabited by coyotes, wolves, foxes,
raccoons, civets, weasels, prairie dogs and prairie chickens,
grouse, bobolinks, meadow larks, and red-winged blackbirds.
On the prairie pink roses grew.

My father, the youngest of ten,
trapped minks, muskrats, beavers, and rabbits.
He hunted pheasants, mallards, and terns.
He netted carps, bullheads, and crawfish.

The land gave forth abundantly
wheat, barley, oats, and flax
from seed they'd brought from Russia.
Then drought, winds, hail, grasshoppers, and blight
took most of it.

In winter they huddled under horsehide blankets
and prayed for spring.

My father married and brought his bride to live
on the homestead with his parents.
Six children were born;
four survived.

I am my mother's last surviving child.
My last surviving memory of my mother
before her death in childbirth
was our planting garden, counting seeds as we buried them
in long, grave-like furrows of dark, rich loam.

And every May I plant a garden, count seeds in grave-like trenches,
pick lilacs, shake mulberries, pull rhubarb, bake bread,
and remember Mother in South Dakota.

ALISON TOWNSEND

*Alison was nine in 1962 when her mother,
Mary, died of breast cancer.*

The Blue Dress

Three months before her death, my father
bought my mother a blue dress at Altman's.
It was a simple shirtwaist,
polished cotton that looked
like a garden at midnight,
sprigs of white and yellow flowers
blooming against a dark blue field.
Tiny ruffles cascaded down the placket,
covering the flat, scarred places
where her breasts had been.

It was the first new dress
she'd had in years besides home-made clothes
she'd sewn from remnants,
and she twirled in it before her children,
blushing, laughing, suddenly a girl again,
the full skirt belling out around her
like Ginger Rogers'
when she danced with Fred Astaire.

It was too late, of course,
though she wore the dress each day
that autumn as if the feel
of it against her body
was like my father's hands.
Still, I love them for buying
that blue dress together.

And when my aunt
said the blue was too dark
to be buried in,
my father insisted,
holding the dress in his arms
the way he'd held my dancing mother,
all the things he couldn't do to save her
wrapped, in a scattering of flowers,
across a dark blue field.

My Mother's Clothes

After the party
that came after the funeral,
when the last neighbors had gone home
with their sympathy, empty casserole

dishes and promises to call soon,
my father asked her sisters
if they wanted her clothes.
He stood in the bedroom

and threw the closet door open,
pulling out her fake fur coat
with the pink satin lining,
a pair of silver party shoes

she'd worn twice, and the row
of homemade dresses she'd sewn,
rick-rack decorations zig-zagging

around the collars and sleeves.
My aunts stepped back as if
he'd struck them, or they could
catch cancer from touching

what once touched her. And the more
my father pressed upon them,
the more firmly they refused, until
I wanted to hurl myself at their feet

and beg them to take something
even if they only threw it away
when they got home. Anything
to stop my father standing there,

her dresses draped in his arms
like the photographs of him
carrying her over the threshold.
But all I could do was stand

in the closet later for hours,
shutting the door, and wrapping
myself in the shape and scent
of what remained of her,

until the pain left and I slept,
and my father found me,
curled under the fur coat,
with the pink satin lining,

my cheek pillowed against
the sparkling silver shoes
he took to Goodwill
the next morning.

The Silver Shoes

The winter before you died
you bought a pair of silver
moire pumps for parties.
They shimmered like moonlight
on water when you walked,
spiked crescents gleaming
beneath the smoky plush of your coat.
But I wore them more than you,
teetering up and down the hall
for dress-up, my arches aching,
your empty rhinestone cigarette holder
flashing in my hand as I pretended to smoke
the Black Cats Daddy brought you from Montreal.

When I slid my feet into your shoes
I was someone who mattered,
their quiet sparkle like starlight
that sometimes salted my dreams.
And you knew to get me my own,
stopping at Wanamaker's on the way
into Grandmother's and saying,
Pick whichever ones you want.

I chose a flower-spangled pair
that fit perfectly in a Ladies five,
their sheen caressing my feet
the way canoes are held by water.
And when my older cousins teased me,
trying the pumps on, asking
could they keep them,
you said, *No they're Alison's.*
She needs them for something.

You never said what for.
But when we got home I asked
if I could try the shoes on
one more time before I went to bed.
You slipped them onto my feet.
I wobbled, a little more certain,
out across the pool of blue braided rug.
The room was nearly dark.
I could not see your face
or guess what you saw
when you looked toward mine,
as I walked away from you
into the shadows, light
sparking out around me
with every step I took.

Black Stone

My first week back at school after the funeral
I found a black stone on the playground at recess.
I was walking alone while the other girls
played jump rope, the familiar rhymes
and slap of the rope against pavement
like a language I'd once known
but stopped speaking when Mrs. Carter
made me stand at my desk
and told the whole fourth grade
to *Give Alison a warm welcome back,*
and tell her how sorry we were
to hear about her mother.

The stone shone out at me from among
faded candy wrappers and old leaves.
I picked it up because it was different
and gave me something to hold on to, perfect
black oval so smooth and warm in my hand.
After that, I carried it everywhere,
deep in the linty cave of my pocket,
or placed carefully under my pillow
where I could reach out and touch it at night.
Once or twice I even held the stone in my mouth,
balancing it on my tongue like petrified music,
wondering what would happen to me if I swallowed.

I planned to have it drilled
or fitted to hang on a gold chain,
like a picture of a locket I'd seen
in a tattered copy of *Godey's Ladies Book*
my mother had found at an auction.
I didn't know then about mourning brooches
or jet cameos carved with faces of the dead.
I just liked rubbing the stone against my cheek,
or holding its slick darkness close to my heart.

I carried the stone all winter,
like a secret I knew so well
I slowly forgot what it meant.
Then one day, when I hadn't reached
to touch it for a while, it was gone.
And though I've looked many times
through books about rocks and minerals,
searching for its name, my stone is never there,

black lake, unblinking eye, lozenge of darkness
that stopped my crying when I held it,
cupped in my palm like a fossilized tear,

polishing its surface till it glowed
with the oil from my own skin,
all the things I couldn't say
bound up in it, hard, black, durable,
permanent as death in my hand.

A Child's Book of Death

I don't know who watched over your body, Mother, after you'd left it, or how my father got you from Cleveland to New York, simply that you arrived, motionless and chilled to the touch as the flesh of certain poisonous mushrooms. I was afraid of you then—though it seemed disloyal—and thought maybe I'd killed you, praying for you to die when you did not return as you'd promised.

Night after night, kneeling beside the spool bed, my pink flannel nightie with lambs tucked around my ankles, the floor breathing snaky drafts, the sisal carpet pricking my knees, I begged the great and implacable dark to make you better and bring you home, offering up Babar or Barbie the way I'd offered Raggedy Ann, on whom I operated, slitting her kapok-filled chest with the nail scissors and digging my fingers in deep for her heart.

Which was supposed to be real, the way you were but then were not, as you lay before us, your body stuffed with darkness I smelled but couldn't see, the distance you'd traveled as enormous as all the states that slept between us while you lay dying in your high, white hospital bed, and Jenny and Steve and I prayed for you—*Our father who art in heaven. . . . Now I lay me down to sleep*—every prayer we knew, our words a useless, innocent gabble we wanted to be true, falling from the small, mint-scented churches of our mouths.

My Mother's Pastels

My mother's pastels came in a thin, green box from France that slid open, its slotted drawer filled with sticks of solid color that looked good enough to eat, words like *fuchsia, chartreuse, bleu celeste* printed on their tattered wrappers, names of colors I had never imagined. "Toutes les nuances du spectre solaire," it said on the label. "All the colors of the rainbow," my mother translated, her voice filling with light the way her face did when she held a pastel in her hand.

Mostly I just looked, but sometimes I tried them out, trading my fat Crayolas and stubby pencils for those wands of pigment and light that grabbed at the page and dusted my fingers with grains of color like pollen. I sat close beside her, moving my hand over the sketchbook the way she did, trying to copy every angle and gesture, pictures of trees flowing from my fingers like water, my mother's translation describing the shivery feeling that came when the world outside fell away and there was nothing but color between me and the page.

She never kept her sketches, but I felt them sometimes, forming out there in a place just beyond my gaze as she plucked chickens, put up tomatoes, bent to put winter chains on the rusty Plymouth wagon that ferried us to school. I don't know exactly what she saw, only the colors she gave me, my hands filled with possibilities for every single page.

Which is why I keep her pastels in my desk drawer, to remind myself how many colors there are in a life, shading in a bright band from red at one end to violet at the other. *Toutes les nuances du spectre solaire.* All the variations of sunlight filtered through the prism of rain. My mother the artist. My mother the 1950's mom. My mother, a woman I will never know, mute and mysterious as the snapshot of her sketching in college, a pastel raised in mid-stroke, the drawing board balanced on her lap like a child.

A Bowl of Sugar

Tonight I prepare apples the way my mother once made them, slender wedges with a bowl of sugar beside them for dipping, grains of glitter clinging, the thinnest line of sweetness sparkling along the outer edge. I don't know why I crave this confection this evening, or why the treat returns, like seasons or the names of apples I ate when I was young— Winesap, Cortland, Northern Spy—except that it makes me a daughter once again in her absence,

as if she stands in the kitchen beside me, the knife flashing, quick as my own long fingers that have grown so much like hers, slicing these near-translucent wafers I take between my lips, letting the grains of sugar dissolve in me slowly, melting against the wet-suede of my tongue, before I swallow and am alone again, the last crickets stitching their music across a cloth of dark that is sweet and unknown to me, yet familiar as sugar, as the girl still standing somewhere inside me, watching to see how it's done.

Margaret was 17 in 1963 when her mother,
Jeanne Buchanan Noonan, died of
cirrhosis of the liver and alcoholism.

Resurrecting Mom

"Mama said there'd be days like this, there'd be days like this, my Mama said."

Who *is* that mother in the song? It is *my* mother in the song we all dance to! She's the best mother in the world, and I've had her all these years. She's the mother everyone wants, but she's mine.

Okay, so she died a drunk when I was seventeen. But imagine she had a chance to sober up. Perhaps it started with a late-night drive to Hazelden. Say I talked her into it and she spent a trying month as Elizabeth Taylor's soul mate. Imagine I had my mother my entire life.

See, I knew it was true! I'm seventeen and there my mother is, stepping through the door of Hazelden. She's walking toward the car and oh! how she glows! You can tell by the way she holds herself that she's ready to be my mother.

What about those cough medicine bottles full of liquor she hides in her alligator bag? Gone! Those times she stands in front of the mirror, tipsy but determined the lipstick would end up only on her lips? Gone! Those icky men I tiptoe out of bed to stare at through the railings on the stairs? Gone! The nights I stayed awake praying she would come home safe . . . but only after my dad fell asleep so he wouldn't kill her? Gone!

See how pretty she looks. She's wearing her pink cashmere sweater, the one with her initials—JBN—spelled in script, in rhinestones, over her right breast. It's my favorite sweater, the soft warm one I love to snuggle up to for a goodnight kiss.

As she gets closer to the car, I can see her eyes are sparkling like diamonds; she's happy to be alive.

I open the door for her. She gets in beside me and says, "Hi sweetheart," then hugs me. She says she's sorry and she cries. She's as brave as a woman on *Oprah*.

When I graduate from high school, my mom pulls me to her and says, "Way to go, kiddo." For everything big and everything happy or sad she's there, wearing her pink cashmere sweater. I'm so lucky to have her.

"I want my mom!" I scream in the labor room.

"I'm here," she says, squeezing my hand. "Breathe."

A beautiful shiny wet baby girl slips out. I'm so tired. I may be a single mother, but I'm not alone. Now I don't have to drag myself out of bed to take care of the baby, time and time again, with no one to help. I fall asleep. My mother cradles her new granddaughter in her arms and tiptoes out of the room. I wake up three hours later, roll over, and drift back to sleep thanking God my mom will stay with me for two weeks.

What would I have done if she had died in that hospital bed in 1963? Who would have given me money for a down payment on my first house, help with my daughter's college tuition, advice to calm me down or put out the fires in my head? I can't imagine.

u

I was seventeen when my mother died. Thirty-four years later, I am at her house having tea. We are laughing about that old flame who broke my heart, old what's-his-name. My mother knows but is refusing to tell.

"Please, Mom! Please, I beg you!"

"Okay, okay. Only if you'll take me to the hairdresser's tomorrow."

"All right. I'll do anything. Now tell me what it was!"

"His name was Jim. Jim Harris," she says. "See you tomorrow."

What a wonderful mother. Tomorrow, after I take her to get her hair done, we'll have lunch and see a movie. I can hardly wait. I knew there would be days like this. I just knew it.

PATTI WAHLBERG

Patti was 18 when her mother, Leona Wojcik,
committed suicide with prescription pills in 1972.

Doom Flower

Mother cats sometimes eat their young.
The weak ones.
Otherwise the babies might suffer
from a blighted bloodline.
So they bear them up to heaven.

I'm almost forty-seven,
the age my mother was
when she took her own life.
Rather than kill me, she left me,
for my own good—
rather than take all of me, she took
just a few small parts—
sent me to the picking fields
with no hands, for instance,
where I stood for years
like a dumb statue,
left me with no voice
to plead my case to the gods
or even to myself in the mute night—

and she took the gods. Drowned them
in her dark bottle,
drank them with her poison.

Now my little girl, at six,
the new recruit,

makes up a silly song about me—
calls it "Doom Flower"—
and it makes me wonder
as I approach this birthday,
if I will allow myself to go
and meet my mother
and allow her
to bear up my release.

Kiss the Dead

I have a tattoo on my forearm
of the end of a cigarette lighter.
It fades in the winter
and comes back with a whack
of nostalgia in the summer sun.

A kiss.

In my dreams I dig up my mother's ashes
and add water. She comes alive
rich and full-bodied like freeze-dried Folgers,
but when the water evaporates,
she always ends up the same.
Dead on her bed
with her arms around
the photos of her little girls,
skinny as a starving kitten,
her face a clay sculpture of pain
at last relieved.

(kiss her clay fingers)

I'm on the verge of spreading her ashes
on the living room carpet
and vacuuming her up with the Eureka.
Or dissolving her in orange juice
like a laxative and drinking her down,
then shitting her out, once and for all.

I want out.

(wait and wait and wait forever
for her mouth to move)

Into the light
with viney roses everywhere
and someone who kisses my tattoos
until they fade away for good
all year long
for all my years.

One Morning at the Mortuary

You notice that the undertaker
looks embalmed;
preserved and white
like he sleeps in formaldehyde.

A huge stiff
suit and stiff white shirt,
a fat slab of meat
with a sleepwalker's glide.

"We want to relieve
as much of the burden

as possible."
He nods and smiles.

Infinite jowls
hang like dead fish;
wax-white hands
are clasped in black lap.

The Angel of Death
(a fairy-ghoul with a magic
hairbrush) appears.
"Did your mother wear her bangs forward or back?"

It doesn't matter, you hear yourself say.
There will be no wake.
"But just in case," comes the pallid response,
"did your mother wear her bangs forward or back?"

You stare at black hairs in the dangling brush
as you picture her just beyond the door
naked on a cement block
her bangs all awry.

It doesn't matter.
"Well, how 'bout forward, then?" and POOF
he's gone to finish painting
red lips on dead white, while

you ponder painting her
back to life,

and the undertaker nods
and smiles.

My Mother's Engagement Ring

My mother's engagement ring is misshapen
where I hammered it to fit my little finger.
It was too small for my ring finger
and just a little too big for my pinky,
so I took a hammer to it

and flattened it just enough to keep it on.
When it's on you can't tell
there's anything wrong with it,
but when it's off, it looks injured.
One side bows out slightly, and the other curves in.

The gold is smooth from the years,
and the little diamond sits in a thick, square setting.
The diamond is tiny. I can see my mother's eyes
fill with tears as she puts it on, blinded by the brilliance
of what it represents to her.

The next day she can't take her eyes off of it,
holding it just so in the sunlight, thrilling
in its flash of color. She's so happy,
she tells herself. She's in love
and the world could not be more perfect.

I wear this ring now.
My eyes fill with tears
when I see it sparkle in the sunlight.
I hammered it to fit my little finger.
I wear it in this imperfect world.

Anna was 16 when her mother, Ruth Virginia
Stauffer Warrock, known as Ginny, died of
cirrhosis of the liver and alcoholism in 1967.

Looking Into Her Death

After my mother's funeral, I begin
looking into her death. I go home.
Is it still home? It feels so,
the carpet green and worn,
the doors hollow and light. I go
into the kitchen. I am sixteen
and thirsty. Is it all right to be
thirsty? It must be. I open the kitchen
cupboard. The glasses, stacked neatly,
become luminous on the shelves.
By opening the door, I shed light
on their curves, their brittleness.
They are so clear I can see the dust
caught on their transparent sides.
Standing there, I realize they are waiting.
The glasses do not know my mother
is dead, so they wait for her hands
to take them down, fill them with
beer or juice or milk, and then
her hands will wash them,
her hands will put them away.
She is dead, I say softly, she is dead.
Outside a bird calls. Her hands are gone.
Suddenly I am afraid that the glasses
will slip off the shelves and shatter,
and I close the cupboard door quickly,

then, after a moment, open it again.
I want them to slide toward me.
Perhaps I'll catch them, perhaps
I'll let them smash. Nothing
moves. The glasses are out of reach.
I close the door, I open it,
I close it, I open it.

Demeter's Daughters

Many women try it, the underworld descent.
What they don't tell you is that there are
two ways down and back. In the first, Persephone,
torn from her mother's side, marries Hades,
eats six pomegranate seeds, and seals her fate
underground. Demeter, her mother, wanders,
wailing to get her daughter back, and then becomes
powerful, and frantic, and succeeds. Persephone
arises. For half the year mother and daughter
reunite, spring returns and the daughter
will reign as Queen of the Underworld.
                              Then there are the others,
the women who pitch forward eager for the dark,
dragging their desires in behind them.

My mother was one of those, ate the pomegranate's
blood juice and kept eating. As a child I believed
she was a goddess, and the hearth she kept
and her song of strength were not a penance,
but her power. "I like it here among the dust and dinners,
see how I like it," she said, nuzzling cold beers
in the suburban living room.

Eager and obliged to serve her,
my sisters and I reflected back her ritual dance.
We took her empty beer bottles to the cellar
and brought up full ones. She never told us
what we were doing. We had to discover
for ourselves. There was a slow falling off,
a cold house to grow into. We served
but could not save her, nor protect her from
the terror of the underground she married.
I grew angry and dark, my sisters pressed themselves
deeper into the rock. And when she had turned inside
to wait for, then give up waiting, then fear the coming
of death, she was crowned. I was sixteen.
                                        I wandered hell alone.
The plague was everywhere, misplaced passion,
and finally exile. I only felt at home
in strange countries, where I listened to the radio
chanting in languages I couldn't understand.
There is more, but so much I have forgotten.
So much is my flesh and bone.
                          Years later, when each spring comes,
I am surprised. Not yet, I say, wait. I want
more time wailing underground, the roots
searching blindly. The bare soil
justifies us, I call it restful.
But I am pulled upright, there is no more waiting.
The bulbs hidden in earth come up, the seeds,
tiny black grit, now put forth green, green. My childhood
was an end like an abyss. Yet I was called up
by a song that rang of blasphemy to my grief:
The year turned. The year turns.
That's the second way. Be prepared.
She dies. I live.

The Outline

In twelfth grade Miss Warren kept me
after English class to ask, Do you know
this paper doesn't make sense?
Puzzled, I looked at my three typed pages
and said, No, I don't know that.
Because she cared, she showed me
how to outline and arrange thoughts.
I'd learned all that younger but had
forgotten the patterns when death
scrambled my bones with my mother's.
Miss Warren and I sat at the oak desk,
and she led me step by step back to reason,
asking what I wanted to say, asking
what I thought might come next.
She would wait a long time in silence,
patiently, because she saw I had to go
a long way off to recollect something
that I thought, that answered the question
and did not signify the impossible, which I
had learned when death took my mother away,
and once I had accepted the impossible,
what was there to say? It disturbed me
to look at the faces of my classmates,
to see their guileless self-absorption.
But when Miss Warren said, A leads to B
leads to C, and you can number inside the letters
1 and 2 and 3, I learned that to think again
was not to betray what I had witnessed,
but to follow a map that led to her oasis,
where she presided with her blond and
gray hair, who had us reading James Joyce
to learn epiphanies, how things come
together or must come apart, and you

can see it in a glance or in the snow.
Later that year, instead of doing drugs or
sitting in a car's back seat with a boy,
I went to Miss Warren's house for tea.
When she asked about my family, I told her
my mother hadn't died of cancer,
like I'd said to everyone, but of alcohol,
and my father was drinking again. Hearing
the truth in her living room, I cried,
and she said, It's a surprise, isn't it, when
you know your family isn't happy. A and
B and C, 1, 2, and 3. Sitting on the sofa,
I knew that stark and brutal outline, and
wanted to fill in the numbers, to frame
my words in this place where, by beginning
to speak, I'd begun to go on.

Interpretive Building

The white letters "Interpretive Building"
are set above two white screen doors
in the brown barn at an Audubon Center.
My mother and I stand in front.
She holds a map.
We are about to take a walk.
Her head half-covers one door,
and mine the other.
It is two years before she will die.
She looks at the camera—
at my father holding the camera—
with a half-smile.
Although I look to her right
and away from mother and father,

I match her half-smile
with one of my own,
lips pressed together,
willing to turn the corners of the mouth
up slightly for the photographer.

I see now that her face is puffy and pale.
Her flowered dress
buttons unevenly down the front,
the cloth straining to cover
her swollen liver.

I didn't see it then.
In the photo, I am fourteen,
wearing jeans and a plaid shirt
buttoned primly to the top.
While the sleeve of the white cardigan
draped over her shoulders
touches my arm,

I look beyond the edge
of her strawberry-blond dyed hair,
away from this day with my parents
into my own world.

My look
into the right-hand distance
is so weary and sad
that I can remember being fourteen.
They had argued the night before,
when, as usual, they had been drinking.

This is my father's way of making up—
take Mama out for the day.
I am along to provide the love.
Maybe they even say they are doing it

for me, and I agree—
unaware that although I think
I am taking care of them,
she is dying.

What is he thinking,
her husband and photographer?
Can he see her illness in her face?
What is she thinking
with her daughter beside her
and her wrinkled dress?
What can she think,
her drinking taking her to a death
she cannot know precisely
but cannot not know?

This single picture
of her last years,
which were not her last years
when we lived them,
holds that day and this.
My grief filters back
until it spreads over the picture
and covers the teenager
looking at the future she
could not possibly have named.
It doesn't matter now,
her ignorance and her anger.
The man and woman are forgiven.
Really not knowing

that he would refuse to see
anything in its true light,
and that she would drink
herself into darkness,

the father took this picture,
and the mother agreed.
They called it
a happy day with their daughter,
as if no one needed to
name or know anything else.

My Mother Sang

My mother sang at the piano,
Cole Porter, Gershwin, the Bumble Boogie,
a rhapsody of melodies for five-, eight-,
nine-year-olds to dance to.
She'd spin us in the kitchen,
fox trot to the Duke
at night, feed our senses
with memories. If she'd married
that boy with a band, where'd we be, now?

We were babies with the blues.
You know the score: she died,
we grew up, and I'm on the edge
of that blue note, ask in a park,
at a restaurant, along the shore,
for that innocent downbeat.
Where'd we be? This is
paradise now, okay?
This is paradise now.

Loyalty

I remember standing with you in the kitchen
the autumn you were ill
and no one talked about it.

Still a teenager, putting my arms around you,
I said that I was glad
you would be a grandmother to my children.

I hadn't known my grandparents.
Having one looked like fun.
And you, Mama, would be a good one.

When you smiled your preoccupied, drifting
smile, you said nothing.
By now the liquor you'd swallowed for years

had made you frail and bloated. When I
hugged you, you moved
my arms to hold my hands in your own.

In five months you were dead.
I knew you were going,
but I had to try my tricks

to make you stay, to make you
suddenly decide to live.
My words could not have worked that change.

But love only wants to be love.
I wanted you to feel
as your love was leaving me, how far and how long

I valued it. I have never had children.
Because of too little
or too much love, Mama?

CINDY WASHABAUGH

Cindy was 12 when her mother, Peggy (Farkash)
Washabaugh, died from acute leukemia.

For Pam, Who Can't Remember

Lean close, little sister and look, because I carry it all
in the glad hump on my back and I'll unpack it for you anytime.

Here, the stretched "o" of your mouth and your
skinny limbs as we clung to Dad when he told us, the way
we flew at him screaming "no" and he held us, 10 and 12, like
we were babies and told us "it'll be all right, we're gonna
be OK," while Grandma stood at the stove crying in the same
small voice she laughed in, making Campbell's Soup
for everyone at 8:45 in the morning because, she said, soup
makes you feel better.

I'll show you the oil Mom painted, how we loved to touch it,
the rough fiber of the paper and the raised brush strokes
sure evidence that she'd been here, that she'd moved
her hands and made a small world of her own that endured.
It was a bright night scene with the black silhouettes of trees
and grass and a full white moon smudging one corner.

One day, I found you brushing your own world onto it
with water colors, so her painting showed through beneath
your translucent swatches; her white moon behind
your pink clouds, her black grass sprouting your flowers
of yellow and red. But the water mildewed the paper a different
black—powdery and reeking of dark things like earth
and coffins—so we had to throw it away.

And because your memory is yet another black—
the black of something so big and so hard that it filled up
the "o" of your mouth that first morning and became
a vacuum in your small skull, swallowing everything around it—
I open this pack for you and welcome you into my own dark
space. I welcome your company in this night lit by so many stars,
each one gleaming its single story, cruel and precious and sweet.

Flying, Gold Night

I pick up my pen and fly on blue words
out of night's starry blur. My daughter calls
for a cup of warm milk. I kiss her cinnamon hair,
longing to hold her safe in this gold night forever.

Out of night's starry blur, my daughter calls.
She wants to know why mothers sometimes die.
Longing to hold her safe in this gold night forever,
I remember a child twenty years before

who wanted to know why her mother had to die.
"Just one last kiss, then it's time for Momma to go."
I was a child twenty years before,
wishing on stars that life could go on and on.

"Just one last kiss, then it's time for Momma to go
for your cup of warm milk." I kiss her cinnamon hair,
learning the rhythms of life go on and on.
I pick up my pen and fly on blue words.

Dream: The Pond

It's two weeks after my mother died and we hear that old Mr. Stanowski next door is trying to kill himself. His son takes away his two shotguns and spends a lot of time at the house with him. One day when his son is getting groceries, Mr. Stanowski takes his straight-edge shaving razor and slashes his wrists wide open. Then he drives his tractor into the pond at the back of his property where we fish. I can't stop wondering whether he drowned or bled to death, though I'm not sure why it matters. An ambulance takes his wife away, her body rotted by years of malignant tumors, though she'd never shown signs of the sickness before. One day, I'm looking into the pond and my mother drives out of it on Mr. Stanowski's tractor laughing. Just this last line is the dream.

Kourtney was two in 1991 when her mother,
Denna Rachelle Wheeler, died from melanoma.

We Never Have to Say Goodbye

Do you know how it feels to lose a parent? I do. My mom died when I was two (that was in 1991). She died of melanoma, a severe type of skin cancer. She was only twenty-seven when she died, but I know she lived a great life.

I have one biological brother named Justin. He was only seven when our mom died. My dad remarried five years after my mom died. He married a woman who also lost her spouse to cancer. Her daughter, Alexandria (my stepsister), was only four when she lost her dad to leukemia, also a severe type of cancer.

I don't know why my mom died and I don't think I ever will, but if I know anything for sure I know that God has helped my family and I through the tough times in life and he still does!

Anyway, a couple of years after my dad married my stepmom they had my half brother, Collin.

God chose to take my mother from me, but in return he gave me a sister, a brother, and a mom!

I thank the Lord that everything turned out okay, and I pray that it stays that way! Oh, and I never had to say goodbye to my mom and I never will, because I know I will see her again in Heaven!

ALLISON WHITTENBERG

*Allison was 18 years old when her mother, Faye
Marlene Whittenberg, died from a heart condition.*

Coats

When my mother was young, she was rich
So rich that her father bought her a coat
Straight from a department store
At ten after closing time by knocking on the window
And shaking a hand full of money at the manager.

It was a beautiful coat
Georgia clay red with a furry collar.

When my mother got a little older, her family was poor
And her mother and she had to share a coat. One had to
Wait for the other to come in order to go out.

It was an ugly coat
Dull, black, dour.

She was neither rich nor poor when she passed away.
My sister and I quarrel over her belongings
One coat particularly.

It was chic
Camel-colored, cinching at the waist.

My father threw salt,
    He said that it looked better on me
    Through persistence, I won it.

She was a secret, mostly silent woman.
What I know of my mother, I glean from shadows.

Rosemary was three when her mother,
Sidney Gay Barnes Wick, committed suicide
with an aspirin overdose in 1970.

4 days before I turned 3

The space between us grows thinner,
perhaps, it never was.

Your family called to say I'm an heir
to an old broken down house
a southern plantation,
with rambling rooms and
a roof in need of repair.
How symbolic,
like parts I inherited,
needing repair too,
after you
checked-out
when I was 2
4 days before I turned 3.

With your absence
there was great room to fill
so, I went seeking
with an insatiable appetite
for spiritual books,
varied terrain
and tender hearts.

A transference took place
and nature became my mother—
the salve to my existential woes.

I found her in the soft island breezes
caressing my cheek,
on mountain tops with rarefied air
and in the giant redwood forests.

Now, I return to the desert
a place you never knew.

The hardest part in losing you
was learning to believe in myself,
at times, an insurmountable wall
defeated me,
voices of doubt trailed me.
Taking care of oneself
was a message I never heard from you.
Unlike the swallows who teach their young to fly,
I relied on others for my flight.

What is your gift?
I was led to delve deeply,
to peer underneath the deluge
of chaos and longing,
emptiness and grief;
to a place
of endless possibility.

If I had received the tender caresses
of your delicate touch
might I have missed the fruits of my own search?

Is it my rational mind,
so insistent upon making fated sense
of unseemly circumstances
that tells me such things?

Now, you are like vapor clouds or photons,
elusive but abundant.
I access you through everything
and still you remain nothing.

ARLENE ZIDE

Arlene was 18 in 1959 when her mother, Goldie
Schwesky Kirschenbaum, died of a heart attack
brought on by her diabetes medication.

Motherless Daughters

What kind of society is it then
that greets with murderous applause
Rambo
as he guns his way through the jungle,
or picks off small-minded small town posses

but walks out in shock when
a truck
  its slimy driver impotently railing from the safety of the sidelines
is pistol-whipped into oblivion
by Thelma
and Louise?

   I search among the threadbare dresses
   for those threads of anger
   tying my throatless voice
   shut
   the slatted blinds
   of tears against an unruly sun

   You left me
   and we had just
   begun

   to speak
   of more than dishes, late night rendezvous

not slamming
the doors
shut.

Unfinished

grief, anger,
rage, resentment,
fear,
abandonment,

mourning still
    —till a hundred and two? . . .

      You weren't there
      when I took over, cooking, cleaning,
      herding the weakling braggadocio males you left behind
      to tend.
      You weren't there.

      I graduated
      alone
      in a circle of college friends,
      daddy, brother, grandmother two
      who never shared a moment of warmth
      with a son's
      daughter

      grandmother one, the one who keened and groaned
      until I doubled over with pain,
      cracked down the middle, I
      could not
      mourn

everyone
came to cry, to feed us mourning
chocolates
we could drown in,
I choked

on chocolate.
You weren't there
when my twin sons were born,
or at my silly wedding.
Everyone

had an opinion
and I was torn.
My new mother-
in-law efficient, calm,
never warm.

You weren't there
when my heart began to mourn
my life, the turn
I'd taken in the wrong road,
the one not taken out of sight
along a vain horizon.
You were gone.

You weren't there
when I needed
you.
You left me, just before my tongue
uncoiled.

What kind of society is it then,
that encourages boys to feel entitled
to women's, girls', mothers', teachers',
everyone's

love?
I too felt like shooting the whole place up,
tearing apart the world that didn't care to have me
speaking out
uncoiling the fire of my witch's tongue

But daughter that I was of yours,
I couldn't,
wouldn't.

didn't.

Contributors' Notes

ELLEN WADE BEALS's poetry has appeared in the magazines *After Hours, Ariel,* and *Whiskey Island* and in the anthologies *Key West, Take Two—They're Small,* and *Family Gatherings.* Poems of hers took second place in Evanston Library's 2003 Jo-Anne Hirschfield competition and third place in the 2004 Frieda Stein Fenster contest. Her short stories have been published in *Willow Springs Magazine* (1999 fiction prize winner) and *Rambunctious Review* (third-place fiction winner). Poems are forthcoming in *Willow Review* and *Quercus Review.* In 2002 she was awarded a residency at the Tyrone Guthrie Centre in County Monaghan, Ireland, to begin work on a novel.

CHRISTINE BOLLERUD has won awards for her humor, poetry, and screenplays. She says, "The death of my mother greatly impacted my life as a writer and a mother, a loss often reflected in my work." "Letting the Goose Run" was published in the *Absolute,* "The Shoebox" in *Story Digest,* and "God's Gargoyle" in *Cholor.*

JEANNE BRYNER has been a practicing registered nurse for more than 25 years and a writing teacher for more than 14. She has won awards for community service, nursing, and writing. To facilitate the healing power of language, she teaches creative writing workshops in cancer support groups, nursing homes, and universities. Her books are *Breathless, Blind Horse: Poems, Eclipse: Stories,* and *Tenderly Lift Me: Nurses Honored, Celebrated, and Remembered.*

JANET I. BUCK is a six-time Pushcart nominee. After receiving her Ph.D., she taught writing and literature for 15 years. Her poetry has appeared in *Octavo,* the *Pittsburgh Quarterly, CrossConnect,* the *Montserrat Review, Offcourse,* the *Pedestal Magazine,* the *Oklahoma Review, Facets Magazine,* and hundreds of journals worldwide. *Tickets to a Closing Play,* her second book of poems, won the 2002 Gival Press Poetry Award, and her third collection, *Beckoned by the Reckoning,* was scheduled for release in spring 2004. Buck's work has been praised for its direct and penetrating approach to grief—be it in relation to her own disability, addiction, or broader issues of social consciousness.

BARBARA M. BURROWS lives with her partner in Northampton, Massachusetts, and works with special needs students in the city schools. Her poetry has been published in *California Quarterly* and *Common Lives, Lesbian Lives*. She is currently working on *White Carnation*, a memoir in verse.

CAMINCHA is from Miraflores, Lima, Peru. She calls the United States her second home and keeps close to her roots—"it is much easier to get where you want to go," she says, "when you are proud of where you came from." In 1987 she earned her M.A. in Spanish literature at San Francisco State University. She was selected by KDTV for its segment *One Of Ours* to honor her contributions to the Latin American community in the Bay Area. Her poems, short stories, and translations have been published in English and Spanish in literary and e-zine magazines. She has also published three chapbooks. The *San Francisco Bay Guardian* has written, "Camincha frames the ordinary in a way that makes it extraordinary, and that is real talent."

JUDITH DANIEL has published in England and the United States. Her work has appeared in *Amhurst Writers* and *Artists and Writers Who Cook*. She is currently at work on a multi-genre work chronicling three generations of her family, celebrating her mother, grandmother, and great-grandmother.

KATHRYN DANIELS was encouraged to put pen to paper early on by her mother, a writer who attempted—with some success—to get published while raising three children and battling chronic illness. Kathryn's poem "Untitled" was selected as one of the 10 best poems of 1980 in *Dark Horse* magazine's Editors' Choice Contest. Her work has appeared in the anthologies *Boomer Girls, If I Had a Hammer, Tokens,* and *Proposing on the Brooklyn Bridge,* among other publications. She lives in New York City.

Susan Elbe wrote her first poem at 10. She says, "Poetry has been a way to nurture myself, a way to cope with the loss of my mother. She was home-nursed by my grandmother the last fourteen months of her life, both a blessing and a curse for her and the family." Susan is the author of a chapbook, *Light Made from Nothing*, and her work has appeared in many journals, including *Calyx, Crab Orchard Review, Nimrod,* the *North American Review, Passages North,* and *Smartish Pace.* She works in Madison, Wisconsin, as a Web content analyst.

Ruby Faulk is a writer living in New York City. She writes for the United Way of New York City and enjoys exploring the many neighborhoods, especially Brooklyn's Carroll Gardens.

Rina Ferrarelli came to the United States from Italy at the age of 15. She has degrees in English from Mount Mercy College and Duquesne University and taught English and translation theory at the University of Pittsburgh for many years. Married, with three grown children, and now writing full-time, Rina likes to read, see plays and movies, and go on long walks. She has published two collections of poetry, *Home Is a Foreign Country* and *Dreamsearch,* and is looking for a publisher for her latest manuscript, *The Bread We Ate.* She is also a widely published award-winning translator.

Anne Foye lives on Nantucket Island, where she teaches poetry and Reiki. Two collections of her poetry and prose poems have been published by Linear Arts Press of Phoenix. She also runs a workshop she created—"Prose to Poems: Writing Towards Healing"—for various community programs.

Laurie Beth Gass, a writer from Holliston, Massachusetts, wrote her first short story in kindergarten. Her piece "For Annie, Clara, Dora and Maybe Sadie" was published in *After Breast Cancer: A Survivors Guide.* Laurie says she used to worry that the loss of her mother—an extraordinary friend, actress, and creative dramatics teacher—was a wound that would not heal. After her mom's death, she nurtured herself by writing more. Now, with a new best friend and still writing, she has survived cancer and the loss of her mother. The wound, however, is still closing.

LAUREN HUDGINS is a student at Reed College in Portland, Oregon. She wrote the poems in this anthology at 17. "Cooled Wax Drippings" is a revised version of a poem Lauren wrote in sixth grade about the last time she saw her mother in her final hospitalization.

RUTH HARRIET JACOBS, Ph.D., lives in Wellesley, Massachusetts. The author of nine books, she is a researcher at Wellesley College Center for Research on Women and a part-time teacher at three colleges. Her memoir, *Women Who Touched My Life,* won the Athena Award in 1998 for a book on mentoring. *Be an Older Outrageous Older Woman* is filled with advice for older women on how to handle finances, health concerns, sexuality, and fun.

JEN CULLERTON JOHNSON's poetry has appeared in *OnionHead, Poetry Motel, Explorations, Coldwater Poettalk, Poet Circle, Amethyst, Nerve Cowboy, nostalgia,* and *Snake River.* Her short stories have appeared in *Poetland Review, Nexus, Co Review, Hampstead Review, LongRoad Review,* and *Sierra Nevada Review.* Jen is bureau chief for the Japan office of the East-West News Bureau and editor at MareNostrum, a bilingual literary journal published in Buenos Aires and the United States.

JOANNE KELLEY lives in Orleans, Massachusetts, and her poems have appeared in *Passager, Sunlight on the Moon,* and *Mourning Our Mothers.*

ELIZABETH KERLIKOWSKE lives and teaches from her home base in Kalamazoo, Michigan. She says losing her mother was the most important event in her life. She has published widely in such magazines as the *Diagram, Redivider, Slipstream,* and *Big Scream.* Her anthology of stories for children, *Before the Rain,* is due out soon from March Street Press.

MIRIAM KESSLER, a mother of four and grandmother of six, has been married for more than 47 years. A retired newspaper reporter and medical transcriptionist, she hosts monthly readings of poetry and prose at the local Camp Hill Diner in Camp Hill, Pennsylvania. Her mother was a beautiful woman. Miriam learned of her mother's death by overhearing a telephone conversation. Her work "When My Belly was Round" was published in *Kalliope,* "Last Supper" in *Feminist Revision and the Bible,* and "All Their Names Were Vincent" in a Simon & Schuster anthology *I Feel a Little Jumpy Around You.* Her book *Someone to Pour the Wine* is a collection of 52 of her poems.

KATHRYN KURTZ has an M.F.A. in creative nonfiction from Goucher College and is a Ph.D. candidate in creative nonfiction at the Union Institute. Her book, *Switchbacks,* is a natural history of the high peaks of the Catskill Mountains.

JEAN LANTIS, a reader and a retired English teacher, started college at the age of 40. She sold 10 articles to *Parents Magazine* long ago, when she was young. In them she wrote about her children, under the pen name Jean Winchester.

SUSAN O'DONNELL MAHAN, of Weymouth, Massachusetts, has been a writer most of her life. In the two years before her mother's death, she wrote two books of fiction; when her mother died, Susan stopped writing. She did not pick up her pen again until her husband died. She has been writing poetry to work through the grief of losing her husband, and now has upwards of 200 poems. She says that Virgina Woolf's statement about her own mother's death—"her death ruined me for everything"—resonates strongly with her. One of the editors of the quarterly *South Boston Literary Gazette,* Susan has two chapbooks of poetry. Her poem "Subway Fantasies" was included in *Tokens,* an anthology of subway poems published in 2003. Several of her poems have appeared in small publications.

TEKLA DENNISON MILLER lives in Colorado. She is a former prison warden who simultaneously managed two prisons—a men's maximum and a multilevel women's—outside Detroit. She also taught children in South Central Los Angeles after the riots, worked with mentally challenged enlisted men while employed with the U.S. Special Services in Germany, appeared on NPR's *Fresh Air with Terry Gross,* and has been featured in many radio, newspaper, and journal interviews. Currently she is a corrections consultant, writer, volunteer, and lecturer. "Lessons My Mother Never Knew She Taught Me" is excerpted from her published memoir, *A Bowl of Cherries.* Her work appeared in *Chicken Soup for the Prisoner's Soul.* Another memoir, *The Warden Wore Pink,* is about her 20-year career in corrections. She has had many nonfiction articles and memoir pieces published in *Fortitude: True Stories of True Grit* and other journals and magazines. She coedited and contributed to *Frontiers of Justice, Volume II: Coddling or Common Sense.* Her first novel, *Life Sentence,* is under contract to Medallin Press with a 2005 release date.

LAURA MOE works as a secondary-school librarian and teaches writing part-time at Ohio University–Zanesville. She says her mother was very funny and dramatic, and that she herself inherited her mother's silly sense of humor, which helps her work with middle-school children. Laura has published a novel, *Parallel Lines* (under the pen name Coyote Gordon), "Women's Words" in *The Virgin #4,* and poems in *Ohio Teacher Write, 5AM, Pudding House,* and the upcoming anthology *Mischief, Caprice and Other Poetic Strategies.*

SHANNON R. NOBLE is a mother of two and a legal secretary. She reads, writes, and otherwise divides her time between worrying about the state of her family and the state of the world. She tries to have faith that her worry is wasted. Her poems have appeared in *Great Poets of Our Time, Verses, Vol. 12, #4,* and *Mirrors, Contemporary Verse From Around the World.*

ANN MURPHY O'FALLON works as a grief and loss therapist and manages the Minnesota Refugee Health Program. Her work as a therapist has been greatly influenced by her mother's illness and death, but even more so by the years that followed. "Trying to successfully integrate that experience has been a lifelong process," she says. She has published numerous professional articles, a few opinion pieces in the *Twin Cities Star*

Tribune, and a short story, "Summer Camp Blues," in *Minneapolis Women.* The mother of three grown children, she enjoys reading, gardening, and warm sunny days. Ann is the coeditor of *Kiss Me Goodnight.*

NANCY SEALE OSBORNE is librarian emerita, State University of New York College at Oswego, and lives in the carefree community of north Fort Myers, Florida. She and her partner have three children and five grandchildren. She canoes weekly with explorer women friends trying to cover the little blue thread lines of Florida's topographical maps. Her grandmother used to want her to go to the cemetery as a child, but she would not because she knew her mother was not there, but in heaven. She has published two biographies, *Crazy Quilt: Funky Smalltown Texas and Other Pieces of Life* and *In the Shadow of a Miracle: Loretto Academy of Our Lady of Light for Girls, Santa Fe, New Mexico.*

MELISSA PALMER lives in New Jersey. Her work "Wails of Grendel" appeared in *University Editions,* "Fire Queen" in *Poetry Motel,* and "Wedding Wish" in Seton Hall University's literary magazine, *Chavez.* Melissa contributed to *Constructions of Widowhood and Virginity,* St. Martin's Press, 2000. She has presented work at both the New Jersey College English Association conference and the International Congress on Medieval Studies. Melissa has completed a novel, *Amelia's Attic.*

DIANE PAYNE teaches creative writing at the University of Arkansas–Monticello. She tells her daughter Ania stories about the grandmother she never met. "Shedding Hair," in this anthology, is an excerpt from her memoir, *Burning Tulips,* which Red Hen Press will publish in the summer of 2004.

CINDY PINKSTON lives in San Jose, California. She says, "My mother has always been a beautiful mystery to me, someone I wish I could remember." Cindy's work "Smiling Skeleton Man" appeared in *Black Buzzard Review,* "Miscarriage" in *Blue Violin,* "Psalm" in *Christianity and the Arts,* "Cooking Lessons" and "The Taking" in *Poetic Matrix,* "Artist" and "Miscarriage" in *ProCreation,* and "Requiem" in *Sunlight on the Moon.*

RACHEL E. PRAY has an M.A. in English (Creative Writing) from San Francisco State University. She lives in Massachusetts with her partner, Laura, and their daughter Talya. A lifelong feminist and activist for social change, Rachel has taught outdoor education, self-defense and literacy, and is trained in Equine Assisted Psychotherapy. Her poetry and photographs have appeared in various publications, including: *Transfer, Mudfish, CQ/California Quarterly, Liberty Hill Poetry Review, Testimony of Lesbian Lives,* and *The Larcom Review: A Journal of the Arts and Literature of New England.* "1983" was a finalist in the National Writer's Union Poetry Competition, judged by Adrienne Rich. Rachel's mother, Ellen M. Egger, was a concert-level pianist, an artist, author, Ph.D. candidate, and mother of three.

REDA RACKLEY lives in Carmel Valley, California, and has an M.A. in cultural mythology. She loves to write and tell stories. She has traveled to West Africa and been trained in the ancient art of cowry-shell divination by an African shaman and is now traveling the world as a diviner. She loves to dance to drums under the moon and howl to the stars in the sky. She has a passion for working with women to explore ancient feminine wisdom using myth, ritual, dance, and bodywork. She is committed to assisting women in fulfilling the dreams their mothers never could. She published "The Circle Continues" in *Women Respond to Circle of Stones* edited by Judith Duerk and "The Return to the Temple—Healing the Feminine Body and Soul" in *Sagewoman Magazine.*

DEIDRA K. RAZZAQUE, a recent Peace Corps volunteer in Costa Rica (in the field of youth development) is currently working toward a M.A. in intercultural service, leadership, and management. Newly married, Deidra, is awaiting the birth of her first child, a daughter. She says, "Planning for my own daughter's birth has made me think of my mother in new ways. As I approach motherhood, I feel more like kin to my mother, rather than just a child mourning her loss. For all the sadness and difficulties it has caused, the early death of my mother also taught me some amazing lessons. I try to appreciate and learn from every experience and each person who comes into my life. I follow my dreams in the moment—there is nothing I will save for the maybe of 'when I retire.' And I never take a day for granted, because I know it may be my last."

LAURA RODLEY has three children, one husband, many ducks, and a variety of other pets. Her work "Acupuncture Love" appeared in the *Massachusetts Review,* "For Cambridge and Somerville" in *Peregrine,* "Morning" in *Sahara,* and other work in *Earth's Daughters* and *Kerf.* She is also a visual artist. Her mother, Sheila Craig Steen, was a research student for Loren Eisley and also coauthored with Anthony C. Wallace "Death & Rebirth of the Seneca," which was published after her death.

DIANA ROSEN is a journalist with countless online, newspaper, and magazine articles, plus 13 nonfiction books, to her credit. Her poems have been published in the journals *RAFFLE* and *convolvulus*; the anthologies *BOLD INK* and *Those Who Can . . . Teach*; and in the books *Time for Tea* and *Winter Tea.* She says, "No matter when our mother dies, it leaves us feeling that part of our life is an unresolved chord, with more to be heard. My poems allow me to relive my most treasured remembrances, those joyful, tender, poignant times, and I hope they give a voice for others who have similar memories."

SAVINA AMICO ROXAS died at 86 in September 2003, while this anthology was in progress. She was a library and information professor at Clarion State University and a teaching fellow in the University of Pittsburgh's Library and Information Science Ph.D. program. Her short stories and poetry have won prizes in various national and local contests. Her memories of her mother are of her as an invalid. After her mother's death, Savina and her four siblings (ages 4 to 12) were raised by their father with no outside help. A tailor, he made most of their clothes. As a result, Savina says, "We were the best-dressed kids in the neighborhood." Her piece "Imperfections" appeared in the *Antigonish Review,* "Peppino's Big Life" in *Paterson Literary Review,* and "Signac, Blvd. de Clinchy, Snow" in *Taproot Review.*

MARJORIE LAGEMANN SNODGRASS grew up in Indianapolis, Indiana; after graduating from Oberlin College in 1950, she taught at Perkins

School for the Blind in Watertown, Massachusetts. In 1952 she married Philip J. Snodgrass, M.D., continuing to teach until the first of four daughters arrived. In 1973 her family moved to her hometown, where she taught at the Indiana State School for the Blind and earned an M.S. in education from Butler University. She also taught visually and multiply handicapped children for 10 years in the Indianapolis public schools. Since retiring, she has written two oral histories: *The First Fifty Years of Arsenal Technical High School* and *Echoes in Retrospect,* an oral history of two decades at Perkins School for the Blind. A member of the American League of Penwomen, she has read her poetry for the Writer's Center of Indianapolis, at church, and for other groups. She is currently writing her memoirs as well as short stories and poetry.

CAROLE STONE is professor of English at Montclair State University in New Jersey. She was a fellow at Hawthornden International Writers Retreat in Lasswade, Scotland, and a fellow at Rothermere American Institute, Oxford University. Her poems appeared in three U.K. journals in 2001: *Smiths Knoll, the North,* and *Poetry Nottingham International.* A poetry sequence, "Postcards from Dublin," was published in *Nimrod International Journal, The Celtic Fringe Issue, 2001.* Other poetry publications include *The Beloit Poetry Journal, The Southern Poetry Review,* and *Chelsea.* Her most recently published poetry books are *Lime and Salt* and *Orphan in the Movie House.*

JENNIFER STONE lives in Berkeley, California. Her selected essays on literature and politics, *Stone's Throw,* won the 1989 Before Columbus American Book Award. Her published works include *Mind Over Media,* essays on film and television; her memoir, *Telegraph Avenue Then;* and a collection of short fiction, *Over By the Caves.* Her weekly radio commentary can be heard on KPFA Pacifica Public Radio, 94 FM, in Berkeley.

LAURIE MICHELLE SUMMER runs a private practice as a speech language pathologist, helping children develop communication skills. She lives with her husband, son, and dog in New Jersey. She regularly participates in open-mike poetry events at local bookstores and cafes, and has been the featured reader at these venues.

ZAHAVA ZOFIA SWEET is a teacher who loves hiking, classical music, and opera. She says, "My mother was the sweetest, most sensitive, and delicate person alive. She endowed me with gifts that never fade. I credit her with my survival." Her piece "The Line" appeared in *Ergo* and in the *Port Townsend Ledger.* "Black Moss" was published in *Semi-Dwarf. Black Crown,* a book of Zahava's selected poetry is soon to be published by Bombshelter Press.

MARIAN KLEINSASSER TOWNE is a retired English and speech instructor, having taught in high schools and colleges in four midwestern states. She continues to garden in Indianapolis and retains ownership of land in South Dakota, where she was first introduced to gardening, farming, and environmental concerns. An activist, she holds membership in the League of Women Voters, AAUW, Church Women United, and the Presbyterian Church. Her publications include *A Midwest Gardener's Cookbook; Bread of Life: Diaries and Memories of a Dakota Family;* and *Jacob Hutter's Friends: Twelve Narrative Voices from Switzerland to South Dakota Over Four Centuries.*

ALISON TOWNSEND is an associate professor of English, creative writing, and women's studies at the University of Wisconsin–Whitewater. She also teaches "In Our Own Voices," a private writing workshop for women. A native Pennsylvanian who lived for many years on the West Coast, she resides in the farm country outside Madison, Wisconsin, with her husband. "I am especially interested in women's writing and writing as a way of healing. I feel that my mother (an artist herself) was the biggest single influence on my creative life." Her poetry and essays have appeared nationally in many journals, including *Calyx, The North American Review, The Southern Review, Nimrod* and *New Letters,* among others. Her work has also been anthologized in a number of collections, including *Boomer Girls: Poems by Women from the Baby Boom Generation, Are You Experienced?: Baby Boom Poets at Mid-Life, Fruitflesh: Ideas for Women Who Write,* and *Claiming the Spirit Within.*

MARGARET NOONAN VAILLANCOURT was born in Alexandria, Minnesota. She remembers her mother as a young, beautiful, wild, loved-by-everyone, flirtatious woman who rarely washed a dish, cooked a meal, or vacuumed a rug. Margaret has been an editor, writer, sailor, community gardener, troubleshooter, pig farmer, and triathlete. Margaret is the coeditor of *Kiss Me Goodnight*.

PATTI WAHLBERG grew up in Massachusetts and now resides in Fountain Valley, California. "I have a whole suitcase full of poems about my mother's suicide," she says. Her poems have been published in *Slipstream, Pearl,* and *Up Against the Wall, Mother.* At 50, with two beautiful daughters and two failed marriages, Patti has found the man of her dreams. She plans to be married (for good) in the fall.

ANNA M. WARROCK writes, "My mother gave me a book of Robert Frost's poetry when I was 11 and a diary at 13, in which I chronicled my father's alcoholism. To chronicle hers would have been a betrayal. I still have both books. When I read some of these poems to audiences, their faces sometimes ripple like waves coming to the shores of grief. My poems have appeared in *The Harvard Review, The Madison Review, Wild Earth, West, Phoebe, Views,* and elsewhere; been performed by a contemporary chamber music ensemble; and been inscribed in brick and installed in the Boston subway. I am a passionate gardener; in a garden death fits with life." *Horizon,* a collection of selected poems by Anna was published in 2004.

CINDY WASHABAUGH is a poet and writer living in Cleveland Heights, Ohio, with her husband, who lost his father as a child. She has a daughter, a stepdaughter, and three cats. "I began journaling and writing poetry at age 12 to ease the grief of my mother's death. The loss of my mother, Peggy Farkash Washabaugh, has had a profound effect on my life choices, especially my choice of career path. I have a B.A. in psychology, a M.A. in creative writing, and a special interest in the use of writing to heal and explore self." Cindy teaches creative writing at Cleveland State University and leads diverse community projects and workshops in the therapeutic art of writing. Her work has appeared in numerous literary journals, most recently in *Poem, Confrontation,* and *Spoon River Review.*

KOURTNEY WHEELER is a high school student in Portland, Oregon. She wrote "We Never Have to Say Good-bye" when she was 12. She loves to play volleyball and hang out with her friends.

ALLISON WHITTENBERG lives and writes in Philadelphia, Pennsylvania. "My mother was a quietly beautiful woman. She never worked outside the home. Originally from the Carolinas, her goal was to marry and have children." Allison's work has appeared in *Virgin Fiction II* (Hearst), *Columbia Review,* and *Pittsburgh Review.* She has produced plays at the Red Eye Theatre, Spruce Hill Theatre, and Theatre in the Round.

ROSEMARY WICK writes, "The impact of my mother's suicide has affected just about every area of my life. It is a tender topic and yet I am working to accept it as a part of my personal myth. According to ancient Greek religion, Athena sprang from the head of her father Zeus; in some ways I've identified with this myth because I have so little memory of my mother. I don't want to characterize her solely by the nature of her exit as the absence of her has given me a kind of strange freedom. I've created an internalized version of an archetypal mother and the feminine principal in all its complexity. Sometimes, as Alice Miller says, the wound is the gift. Rosemary is a painter and is nearing completion of a master's in counseling.

ARLENE ZIDE, born in New York City, has a Ph.D. from the University of Chicago in linguistics and South Asian languages and civilizations. A former editor of *Primavera,* she is currently putting together an anthology of Chicago area women poets, *Chicago Fire,* with Carolyn M. Rodgers. Her work has been published in many journals in the United States, in Canada, and in India, including *Xanadu, Rattapallax, Primavera, Colorado Review, Meridians, A Room of Her Own, Oyez, Off Our Backs,*

Rhino, Parnassus Literary Review, and *The Women's Review of Books.* She has spent a good part of her adult life in India. She is currently professor emeritus of humanities and women's studies at the City Colleges of Chicago. She says, "My mother's death is the one thing I have never really been able to 'get over.'"

Permissions

We are grateful to the authors who have given us permission to include previously unpublished work in this anthology. We also thank the authors and publishers who have given us permission to reprint previously published work.

"August 1999: Light Is a Measure of Time" has not been published and is printed here with permission of the author, Ellen Wade Beals.

"The Mother Thing" and "It's just a purse but . . ." have not been published and are printed here with permission of the author, Christine Bollerud.

"Fairies Live in the Next Town" was published in *Eclipse: Stories* (Bottom Dog Press, 2003) and is reprinted here with permission of the author, Jeanne Bryner.

"Aching Vacancy" was previously published by *The Green Tricycle*. Copyright © 2000 by Janet Buck and reprinted with permission of the author. "This Is How I Like My Eggs" was published by *The Muse's Kiss,* Summer 2001. Copyright © 2001 by Janet Buck and reprinted with permission of the author. "Wild Horses, Sugar Cubes" has not been published and is printed here with permission of the author, Janet I. Buck.

"Before My Birthday" has not been previously published and is printed here with permission of the author, Barbara M. Burrows.

"An Announced Death" has not been previously published and is printed here with the permission of the author, Camincha.

"A Mirror and A Photograph" has been published as a broadside in London. Copyright © Judith Daniel and reprinted here with permission of the author, Judith Daniel.

"At the End," copyright © 2000 by Kathryn Daniels, "Litany," copyright © 1999 by Kathryn Daniels, have not been published and are printed here with permission of the author, Kathryn Daniels. "Untitled" has been published by *Dark Horse Poets* (1980) and is reprinted here with permission of the author, Kathryn Daniels.

"My Mother Isn't Dead" has not been published and is printed here with permission of the author, Susan Elbe. "At My Mother's Bedside" first appeared in *North American Review* (September–October 2004) and is reprinted here with permission of the author, Susan Elbe.

"The Rabbit Chase" has not been published and is printed here with permission of the author, Ruby Faulk.

"I Remember, or Do I?" has not been previously published and is printed here with permission of the author, Jean Lantis.

"World View" was published in the chapbook *Paris Awaits,* 2002. Copyright © 2002 by Susan O'Donnell Mahan and reprinted here with permission of the author, Susan O'Donnell Mahan.

"Lessons My Mother Never Knew She Taught Me" is an excerpt from the author's memoir *A Bowl of Cherries* (PublishAmerica, 2001) and it is reprinted here with permission of the author, Tekla Dennison Miller.

"After" was published in *The Ohio Poetry Day Association,* 2001. Copyright © 2001 by Laura Moe and reprinted here with permission of the author, Laura Moe. "Living Room" has not been published and is printed here with permission of the author, Laura Moe.

"Hurt," copyright © 2001 by Shannon R. Noble, has not been published and is printed here with permission of the author, Shannon R. Noble.

"Lilacs," copyright © 2004 by Ann Murphy O'Fallon, has not been published and is printed here with permission of the author, Ann Murphy O'Fallon.

"Orange-Red Indian Paintbrushes" was published in the author's memoir *Crazy Quilt: Funky Smalltown Texas and Other Pieces of Life* (Hale Mary Press, Inc., 1999) and is reprinted here with permission of the author, Nancy Seale Osborne.

"Mom's Song" and "Things I forgot to tell you, too" have not been published and are printed here with permission of the author, Melissa Palmer.

"Shedding Hair" was published in *Toast* (1995) and *Shards Anthology* (1999). Copyright © 1995 by Diane Payne and reprinted here with permission of the author, Diane Payne.

"Inheritance" has not been published and is printed here with permission of the author, Cindy Pinkston.

"1983" has not been previously published and is printed here with permission of the author, Rachel E. Pray.

"The Grapefruit" has been told many times by the author, but it has not been published. It is printed here with permission of the author, Reda Rackley.

"What Remains" has not been published and is printed here with permission of the author, Deidra K. Razzaque.

"Bearings" has not been published and is printed here with permission of the author, Laura Rodley.

About the Authors

Margaret Noonan Vaillancourt and **Ann Murphy O'Fallon,** the editors of *Kiss Me Goodnight,* were both children when their mothers died. Ms. O'Fallon is a licensed psychologist whose counseling work focuses on grief and loss. She also coordinates Minnesota's Refugee Health Program. Ms. Vaillancourt is a writer, triathlete, and community activist. She also owns a vintage clothing store with her daughter. Both Ms. O'Fallon and Ms. Vaillancourt live in Minneapolis, Minnesota.

To order additional copies of *Kiss Me Goodnight*:

Web: www.itascabooks.com

Phone: 1-800-901-3480

Fax: Copy and fill out the form below with credit card information. Fax to 651-603-9263.

Mail: Copy and fill out the form below. Mail with check or credit card information to:

Syren Book Company
c/o BookMobile
5120 Cedar Lake Road
Minneapolis, Minnesota 55416

Order Form

Copies	Title / Editors	Price	Totals
	Kiss Me Goodnight / **O'Fallon & Vaillancourt, eds.**	$16.95	$
	Subtotal		$
	7% sales tax (MN only)		$
	Shipping and handling, first copy		$ 4.00
	Shipping and handling, ___ add'l copies @$1.00 ea.		$
	TOTAL TO REMIT		$

Payment Information:

___ Check Enclosed ___ Visa/MasterCard	
Card number:	Expiration date:
Name on card:	
Billing address:	
City:	State: Zip:
Signature :	Date:

Shipping Information:

___ Same as billing address ___ Other (enter below)	
Name:	
Address:	
City:	State: Zip: